JB JOSSEY-BASS™
A Wiley Brand

T0304595

Nonprofit Publications

What You Need to Know to Create Winning Publications

Scott C. Stevenson, Editor

WILEY

978-1-118-69195-3   ISBN

978-1-118-70407-3   ISBN (online)

Nonprofit Publications

What You Need to Know
To Create Winning Publications

Published by

Stevenson, Inc.

P.O. Box 4528 • Sioux City, Iowa • 51104
Phone 712.239.3010 • Fax 712.239.2166
www.stevensoninc.com

Nonprofit Publications: What You Need to Know to Create Winning Publications.
Edited by Scott C. Stevenson.
© 2010 Stevenson, Inc. Published 2010 by Stevenson, Inc.

Nonprofit Publications What You Need to Know to Create Winning Publications

USEFUL POLICIES, GUIDELINES AND PUBLICATION PROCEDURES

What policies and procedures do you have in place that address various aspects of communications, publications, community relations and more? The time and thought you put into planning procedures, developing guidelines, addressing and approving policies and so forth will make for a more smoothly running operation. When new staff are hired, they will have a map to guide them. When issues arise, you will have board-approved policies to which you can turn.

Use Editorial Calendars to Track Important Publication Dates

An editorial calendar can streamline your publication process by tracking important publication tasks and dates and by keeping your publishing staff on schedule and on target.

The International Code Council (Country Club Hills, IL), for example, has used an editorial calendar for all print and online publications during the past four years. The calendar keeps staff focused on crucial publication deadlines.

Steve Daggers, communications vice president, says the editorial calendar lists all deadlines, themes and publishing dates. It even includes special sections for copy deadlines, advertising insertion deadlines, printer deadlines and mailing dates.

The council gathers information from staff members through e-mail and face-to-face communications. They also use the calendar to track comments received from readers and advertisers, as well as online surveys. They work backwards from the publication date, taking into consideration when publications must be reviewed and printed.

The council also undertakes weekly conference calls with all departments (20-plus people). These calls encourage broad input, while serving as a reminder of deadlines included on the calendar.

The editorial calendar is compiled during the June-August period. It is viewable online by all staff members, but change requests must be channeled through the editors. The editorial calendar is also included in the council's media kit. "It's a service to our advertisers, so they know the timelines and can plan their ad buys accordingly," says Daggers.

Editorial Calendar Benefits

Daggers shares additional benefits of an editorial calendar:

1. Everyone is aware of the communications department's plans when they submit material for publication.

2. Other departments know that if they want to get the word out about an issue, they can check the editorial calendar and see where it might fit in.

3. The whole organization can view the calendar on the Web, eliminating the need for repeated updates to the publishing staff.

4. The organization is spread across four time zones, but the calendar can be accessed at any time from any location.

Source: Steve Daggers, VP Communications, International Code Council, Inc., Chicago District Office, Country Club Hills, IL. Phone 1-888-ICC-SAFE (422-7233) ext 4212.

2007 PRODUCTION SCHEDULE
Building Safety Journal and Building Safety Bulletin

Content not available in this edition

Matrix Helps to Guide Creative Process

Save time by creating communications tools that help organize and simplify projects.

Danielle Kessler, director of marketing programs, Wheaton College (Wheaton, IL), says, "When I work with clients who need to produce multiple publications centered on an event or project, I often draw a matrix that essentially lays the individual pieces, target markets, delivery systems and responsible parties over a calendar. Intentionally less detailed than a project management or scheduling tool, which helps track related tasks, this simple document serves as an overall guide for the creative process. Without it, budgets are difficult to determine and opportunities can be missed."

The matrix idea can be adapted to suit any nonprofit communications office. Depending on the scope of projects involved, a well-planned template can be used for all projects.

Kessler details the process of creating a matrix:

The matrix shown here guides the creative process when producing multiple publications.

- Creative staff meets with the client to discuss elements of the matrix or map.

- Staff puts information into matrix format and sends a copy to the client.

- Client uses matrix as a reference point as they initiate the individual marketing activities.

- Creative staff use the matrix to plan for an efficient workflow and to use as a reference point as individual activities are initiated.

Source: Danielle Kessler, Director of Marketing Programs, Wheaton College, Wheaton, IL.

Content not available in this edition

Simplify Your Job Through Style Guides

Ever have one of those days where it feels like all you did was approve copy, verify logo usage and try to get people to just use your name right? The back-and-forth that keeps your brand intact can be maddening. But a style guide can save the day.

A basic style guide gives people clear guidelines for how to present your organization. The more you add to your style guide, the fewer questions you will get. Style guides also give you a consistent image in the media.

So what should you include? Choose from the following list to create a style guide that works for your organization.

Tedious as they can often be, a basic style guide offers a clear and consistent procedure for how to present your organization.

✓ **Proper name usage.** Include correct hyphenation and capitalization plus any regional or chapter-specific designation if appropriate.

✓ **Proper logo usage.** Include correct color plus size and white space designations.

✓ **Print and design instructions.** You may want to include the proper mix for a Pantone color or other specific design guidelines such as preferred font and size.

✓ **Appropriate language.** Are there words your organization does or doesn't use about its work or its clients? Do you phrase things in a certain way? Make sure people know that.

✓ **Boilerplate information.** Include your mission, a positioning statement and any relevant, updated statistics.

Be sure to include contact information for the person who should receive questions and give final approval. A style guide should not replace staff review of materials; it should simply streamline the approval process for all involved.

Guidelines Simplify Design Process

Compiling a concise list of proofing rules will streamline the approval process.

Staff at Loyola University New Orleans (New Orleans, LA) use a required checklist for proofing/approving projects. Created by Loyola's former marketing director in the 1990s and updated as needed, the checklist (below) is part of a policy and procedures booklet sent to all faculty and staff and available on the university's website.

"Our clients understand these policies require their involvement throughout the project, including their final approval, which creates a win-win for us all," says Mary Degnan, publications manager.

The checklist contains 10 guidelines that pertain to all written materials.

When creating a set of guidelines, Degnan advises including common-sense rules, like using spellcheck or checking for continuity, as well as logo use restrictions, color/font preferences and other branding rules.

Keeping a list to 10 key points is preferable since it is easy to read and remember; however, some situations may require you to go beyond to cover all of your organization's policies.

Source: Mary Degnan, Publications Manager, Loyola University New Orleans, New Orleans, LA. Phone (504) 861-5884. Website: www.loyno.edu

A policy and procedures booklet (shown here) is shared with all employees of Loyola University New Orleans.

Content not available in this edition

Publication Guidelines Foster Consistent Message

Creating design and style guidelines will lead to a consistent look for your materials.

When Tammy Whaley came on as director of university communications for the University of South Carolina Upstate (Spartanburg, SC) in 2002, the university had no review/approval guidelines. Various departments were producing their own materials, often using the logo incorrectly, misspelling words and not representing the university in the best image, she says.

So Whaley formed a communications roundtable to engage the campus community in communication-related topics, including appropriate and approved usage of logos, an editorial style guide and graphics standards manual, all aimed at effectively branding the university and creating a consistent message.

Among the roundtable's first acts was to create and implement a review and approval process (see box).

Comprising 17 people from various departments, the roundtable met every two weeks until the process was approved, and monthly after that. Whaley met with directors of the printing services and purchasing departments to get their buy-in and cooperation. Then the roundtable rolled out the plan on campus.

"The whole process took less than two months," says Whaley. "We (the PR office) had a good idea of what we thought needed to be included, but once the group met and started talking, we realized the items covered needed to be expanded."

Materials that need to adhere to the guidelines include university event materials, recruitment materials, Web page copy and photos, advertisements and printed materials for campus-wide and off-campus distribution. The PR office asks for a minimum of 48 hours lead time to review documents.

A key component in implementing such guidelines is educating all staff on how the guidelines work and the importance of adhering to them, she says.

The office of university communications explains the guidelines at new faculty orientations, Whaley says. "We explain the role of our office and show samples of work we have done for other departments and faculty members on campus.

"Once faculty sees the level of professionalism that comes out of our office — whether it is for a newsletter, brochure or magazine — they are much more inclined to let us get involved in the project than trying to do it themselves using desktop publishing."

In cases where staff do not adhere to guidelines, Whaley says, "I contact the person who submitted the project and explain why the project doesn't meet the guidelines and work with them until the project is brought into compliance."

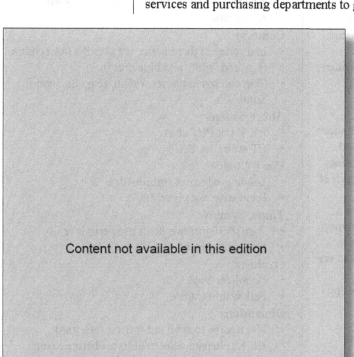

Content not available in this edition

This process helps guarantee consistent, quality publications for the University of South Carolina Upstate (Spartanburg, SC).

Since establishing the guidelines, Whaley says, "The campus community has become much more educated on correct logo usage, correct PMS usage (Pantone Matching System — a color chart used to match exact colors) and adherence to the guidelines. The university's publications have certainly improved in terms of higher-quality design, presenting a consistent look and creating a brand that is easily recognizable."

Source: Tammy E. Whaley, Director of University Communications, University of South Carolina Upstate, Spartanburg, SC. Phone (864) 503-5210. Website: www.uscupstate.edu

Style Sheets Ensure Consistency

Finding innovative ways to ensure that your organization is consistently communicating information on all fronts is crucial to outreach and branding efforts.

Denise Rader, director, media relations, St. Luke's Hospital & Health Network (Bethlehem, PA) explains. "A style sheet is a set of communication standards that dictates how organizations prefer to present written material to the public. An example of a style sheet is the AP Stylebook that journalists use to check common uses of words, titles, phrases, places and commonly misused or misspelled words. Style sheets help an organization communicate consistently, no matter who is writing."

St. Luke's utilizes both an internal and external style sheet; the latter being listed on the organization's website for the past three years. Rader says, "St. Luke's has both an external style sheet, which is posted on the website for the media to use, and an internal style sheet, which is used by the marketing professionals in the St. Luke's Hospital & Health Network marketing/communications department to standardize our written communications. For example, we use 'health care' as two words, instead of 'healthcare' as one word."

Rader says, "The sheet provides the correct name designation of our facilities and provides links to many of those sites. The listing helps maintain awareness of the depth and breadth of our organization, clearly demarcates our affiliations, creates/maintains brand awareness and exemplifies the reach of our excellent services."

Evaluate your communications practices to see where a style sheet may have the most impact. "Your organization may be inconsistent in its communication practices," says Rader. "Look at inconsistencies in your written communications to see which areas need to be standardized."

When developing a style sheet, Rader recommends using the AP Stylebook as the main reference.

Rader says, "Style sheets help to standardize communications, which is very important in order for your brand messages to be repeated enough to build or maintain your name recognition. It helps to reduce spelling errors and to ensure that your organization's name is spelled correctly at all times. The style sheets may provide additional ideas for stories and an easy way to access more information through your website links."

While a style sheet can serve as a valuable tool, ensuring the information is both accurate and usable is vital. "For organization-specific words and phrases, before you include it on a style sheet, make sure you can live with it. Obtain support from senior managers prior to implementing a style sheet. Share it internally with everyone who generates letters or communicates with the public in any way. Every letter or piece of printed material in the organization should adhere to the style sheet," says Rader. "If you create a style sheet, use it! Consistency is key."

Internal Style Sheet Sampling

"The internal style sheets are used by the marketing department of 10 people, as well as the vice president of corporate communications," says Rader.

It includes the following:
- St. Luke's Hospital & Health Network (use ampersand and not the word "and")
- A listing of titles and credentials (e.g., John Smith, MD or Mary Jones, DO or Suzy Miller, RN, MSN) not using periods and listing people with titles (e.g., Denise E. Rader, Director, Network Media Relations, St. Luke's Hospital & Health Network (name, title, department, organization)

Commas
- In a series of three items, we skip the last comma (e.g., red, white and blue dress)
- Skip comma in names with Jr. (e.g., Sr. John P. Smith Jr.)

Abbreviations
- P.E.T. not PET scan
- CT scan (not CAT)

Word Choice
- Leading-edge not cutting-edge
- Preventive not preventative

Times, Symbols
- 7 am, 6:30 pm (we don't use periods or 00)
- Spell out percent

Hyphens
- Board-certified
- Fellowship-trained

Dimensions
- Use figures to spell out inches, feet, yards, etc. Hyphenate adjectival forms before nouns: (e.g., He is 5 feet 6 inches tall. Or the 5-foot-6-inch man.).

Ages
- Use figures (e.g., 5-year-old boy)

Addresses
- Use abbreviations when number is available, but spell out when there is no number (e.g., 1900 Pennsylvania Ave. or Pennsylvania Avenue)

Capitalization
- A reminder of trademarked names that must be capitalized
- Names of departments must be capitalized
- X-ray (capitalize X)
- Internet not internet

Source: Denise E. Rader, Director, Media Relations, St. Luke's Hospital & Health Network, Bethlehem, PA.
Phone (610) 954-4104. E-mail: raderd@slhn.org

Create Writers' Guidelines for Would-be Contributors

Does your organization publish any newsletters, magazines or journals to which other authors might submit articles? If so, it's wise to have writers' guidelines available for those who are interested.

Here's a checklist of items to include in your newsletter's writers' guidelines:

✓ The type and size of articles you're looking for. Do you want feature stories? Tips and ideas? Events and calendar items?

✓ What graphical elements are needed (photos, artwork, etc.) and in what format (JPEG, TIFF, etc.).

✓ Who will retain copyright to the article.

✓ What your style requirements are. Does your publication follow the Chicago Manual of Style? AP Stylebook? What specific style requirements do you have (e.g., website instead of Web Site; e-mail instead of email; etc.)?

✓ Whether you want to receive query letters or full manuscripts. How you want to receive submissions (e-mail or mail or both), in what format and to which address.

✓ How much you will pay for each article and when. Will you pay a standard fee of $50 per article; 25 cents per word; etc.? Will you pay upon acceptance or when the article is published?

Bios Made Easy

Does your office produce biographies of board members, employees, customers and others? To make the job easier, develop a basic questionnaire you can send (or e-mail) to those on whom you need biographical information. Incorporate some open-ended questions that reveal some personal attributes: hobbies, opinions and such.

Include a self-addressed envelope or ask them to e-mail the survey back as an attachment.

Let Clients, Volunteers, Donors Tell Why in Their Own Words

Looking for a procedure you can follow to collect genuine testimonials? Consider this idea. Produce a fill-in-the-blanks template that constituents — clients, former clients, donors, sponsors — can use to guide them in describing their perceptions of your organization in their own words.

Create a form such as the one shown here and distribute it to particular groups of individuals as opportunities arise: receptions, seminars, in mailings. As you get the completed forms back, select those you like best and use the actual form as a testimonial in printed materials — along with a photo of the individuals.

A template such as the example shown here can make it easier for friends and supporters of your organization to offer genuine testimonials.

Mike and Susan Melrose believe XYZ Nonprofit merits their support. Do you? If so, we'd love to hear why — in your own words!

Mike and Susan Melrose Photo Here Along with brief bios/quotes as to why they support XYZ nonprofit.

XYZ Nonprofit is important to me/us because _____

_____

I/we choose to support this organization because _____

I/we really believe you ought to consider investing in XYZ Nonprofit, too! Here are just a few reasons why:

_____

_____

_____

When Flyers Aren't Up to Standard

A staff member or volunteer throws a bake sale, jump-rope-a-thon or other event on your nonprofit's behalf. The idea is wonderful and money welcome, but the flyer is below your standards, perhaps even sending the wrong message to the community.

What to do? How you react to an amateurish or inappropriate flyer for an event benefiting your organization depends on when you encounter it.

- **Proactive**: If you run across the flyer before it is distributed or when most can still be intercepted, by all means, run an interception! Tell the bearer "I bet we'll get more response if we put this in our standard flyer format so people have no question that it benefits our cause. How many copies do you need?"

- **Reactive**: If you don't hear of the event until flyers are posted, it's perhaps best to let it go — this time — as long as information is factual and the event appropriate. Tell organizers you will do a press release on agency letterhead and story for in-house publications. Then add: "In the future, it would really help both the event and our cause if flyers/news releases/promotions came out of our office. We want to give a consistent message to the community. Call us and we'll work together!"

- **Preventive**: Establish a policy on special event promotion and communication. Post it on your intranet for staff. Provide a PDF or Word document they can access, input specifics and print. Or create and make available a generic preprint with specifications of how to add text to create flyers that meet your standard.

Content not available in this edition

A generic flyer template such as this can help send a consistent message and reassure the audience that the event is actually supported by your organization.

Provide Clear Guidelines for Story Submissions

Many organizations allow constituents to submit story ideas via their website. Mercy College (Dobbs Ferry, NY) goes a step further to include nine questions with its online Submit a Story Idea form to help users determine if their stories are newsworthy.

"The nine questions that determine news value were included to assist our various constituencies, both internal and external, in better understanding what we look for and how we measure newsworthiness within our department," says Christine Baker, director of public relations. "They are straightforward and help to define the information before it is submitted to our office."

The questions include:

- Does the information have any importance to the reading, listening or viewing public?
- Do you have a new angle on an old story?
- Would the audience pay to know the information?

Baker and her colleagues spend minimal time directing people to the list as most users are familiar with it, she says. "Our internal constituencies really know this information since we have developed relationships with so many faculty and staff already. For our external constituencies, such as alumni and friends, they typically find the newsroom on their own and submit story ideas to us. While we rarely direct external audiences to that page, we know they are finding it because of the story ideas we receive and follow up in our office."

For organizations considering a similar online tool, Baker offers this insight. "As public relations professionals, I think it is important for us to remember that not everyone thinks about those questions before submitting an idea. Further, it helps explain to those who may not know what we do, why we request certain information."

Source: Christine Baker, Director of Public Relations, Mercy College, Dobbs Ferry, NY. Phone (914) 674-7596. E-mail: cbaker@mercy.edu

In addition to inviting story submissions, help participants determine, in advance, if their stories are newsworthy.

Nonprofit Publications: What You Need to Know to Create Winning Publications.
Edited by Scott C. Stevenson.
© 2010 Stevenson, Inc. Published 2010 by Stevenson, Inc.

Nonprofit Publications What You Need to Know to Create Winning Publications

TIPS FOR PRODUCING STAND-OUT ANNUAL REPORTS

Although nonprofit organizations may not be required to produce an annual report as publicly-traded companies are expected to do, there are many reasons for publishing and distributing an annual report to your shareholders: board members, donors, volunteers, those you serve and have served in the past and more. Your annual report should provide a summary of the past year that addresses both achievements and challenges. It should serve as the window to your organization.

Go Beyond Expected for Stand-out Annual Reports

Is your organization's annual report a necessary evil covering basic financials and the obligatory chairman's letter? You may be missing an opportunity to highlight your programs and update your base about the year's important developments.

Here are some strategies for giving your annual report some broad appeal.

As much time and effort as it takes to produce an annual report, be sure you're producing a report that captures people's attention and gets read.

✓ **Spotlight fundraisers and events.** Use the best photo from each one with a brief report on amounts raised, attendance and a brief overview of its purpose. Even in black and white, photographs and results draw people into your message.

✓ **Put a human face on your programs.** Choose one or two stories about individuals or families your programs helped during the year to show supporters and donors the positive effects of their support in a personal way.

✓ **Look for ways to creatively handle dry facts and figures.** You may be required to report financials that are dull to many readers, but you can either keep them separate from more appealing news, or illustrate them with photos related to each category. Simple pie charts and graphs may encourage some to check out the section and learn more about your operations.

✓ **Recognize your board and leadership.** Use a group photo or head-and-shoulders shot for each one with brief biographies. This is an opportunity to show broad community support for your programs.

✓ **Make chairman's or president's letter a meaty one.** When you must include this, make it a brief overview of the year's successes and challenges, and outline goals for the year ahead. Include a message of gratitude for staff, volunteers and donors.

✓ **Don't forget to include contact information and your event calendar.** When your annual report lists staff or board contacts, program and service locations and a schedule of important events for the year, people will save it and perhaps even continue to read it for months.

Invigorate Your Annual Report With a Theme

Looking to breathe new life into your annual report? Consider incorporating a theme into it.

"A theme is a great way to garner interest, but it's also a great tool to guide a reader through the publication. We can establish an introductory soft story to get them started. Then build up to the middle with some drama and conflict, then bring them down with some stories about future plans and how they can help," says Siobhan Carlile, assistant director of development, manager of communications, Augusta Preparatory Day School (Martinez, GA).

It can serve as a refreshing change for your readers and is a great way to generate excitement about your report.

Don't overlook the possibility of incorporating a theme into your organization's annual report.

"A theme keeps a feel of consistency and builds a relationship between stories. In the case of service it shows that we aren't just giving lip service about philanthropy and community service, but that we practice it sincerely. We have made it a priority and it's part of our culture," says Carlile.

Creating a theme can also give your organization a new way to approach compiling the report. "Themes evoke emotions, feelings, memories. Who doesn't want to touch their audience?" says Carlile. "We aspire to making our annual report an event for the reader, something pleasant and memorable. It is just a snapshot of what we do during the year; we want it to be clear, concise, accurate and above all leave the reader feeling like, 'Yes, I knew I wanted to support them; it was the right decision.'"

Source: Siobhan Carlile, Assistant Director of Development, Manager of Communications, Augusta Preparatory Day School, Martinez, GA. Phone (706) 863-1906 ext 214.

Let Your Mission Guide Your Theme

When using your mission as inspiration for your annual report, find a variety of ways to highlight your organization's goals and accomplishments.

Wendy Romano, director of marketing and communications, Philadelphia College of Osteopathic Medicine (Philadelphia, PA), explains: "Our mission drives the choice of themes for our annual report. Each theme harkens back to an element of our mission. Our annual report theme reinforces the college's annual strategic plan and highlights successes of the plan as well."

A mission-inspired theme will help ensure that your annual report illustrates the importance of the work you do. "A strong theme helps us structure our annual report, while making it easier to reach a busy readership. Critical issues are highlighted and reinforced through the theme."

A theme is an excellent way to highlight specific events and accomplishments from the previous year, to remind your community about your mission and to emphasize fidelity to the mission. "Our annual report details events, accomplishments and other developments in a precise manner and in compliance with financial reporting requirements. However, it also solidifies forward-looking plans for efforts rooted in our mission," says Romano. "Each report focuses on the college's dedication to the education of students in medicine, health and behavioral sciences. Feature stories — often human interest pieces tied together by the theme — portray our institution's commitment to teaching, research, the osteopathic tradition, leadership, service and the well-being of the community."

Past annual report themes included: Synergy (2006); Cultivating Growth (2005); and Inspiration Comes From Within (2004). All departments involved in the process were aware of the importance of commitment to the chosen theme. "It is important that parties involved communicate throughout the publication process. Key players are always included in the initial marketing and communications meeting and are encouraged to adhere to the theme when contributing to the report."

How is a theme selected? "The report is prepared by a core staff. Once ideas are proposed and honed by this group, recommendations are shared with various campus departments and eventually with the president and his senior cabinet. The report staff works hand-in-hand with administration to ensure thematic messages are ingrained in the minds of core constituencies, including writers, designers, photographers and printers. Standard topics such as development/ scholarships; academic and clinical education; research; and campus expansion projects must be dealt with in a consistent and straightforward manner."

Recognize that a mission-inspired theme will help ensure your annual report illustrates the importance of the work you do.

Sources: Wendy W. Romano, Director of Marketing and Communications, Philadelphia College of Osteopathic Medicine, Philadelphia, PA. Phone (215) 871-6300. Jennifer Schaffer Leone, Communications Manager, Philadelphia College of Osteopathic Medicine, Philadelphia, PA. Phone (215) 871-6303.

Content not available in this edition

Content not available in this edition

Content not available in this edition

Five Ways to Showcase Your Organization's Stories

The larger your nonprofit's scope, the greater the potential for great stories about the people you touch. To identify subjects and people to generate the coverage your organization deserves:

- ❑ **Be a historian.** Familiarity with your organization's past helps you discover links to its future. It may have a long history of programs supporting women's issues, child advocacy, helping laid-off workers find new careers or other timely topics. Pave the way for an article about your organization's pioneering spirit and continuity of mission.

- ❑ **Get into the trenches.** Shadow your staff or volunteers for a few days. See what they do for people your organization serves, and get to know some of those who benefited, like the young single mother who found a good job through one of your programs or the great-grandmother who is enjoying needlepoint again because of new eyeglasses you provided.

- ❑ **Ask supporters for ideas.** Your newsletter or website is a great vehicle for asking supporters to tell you about a good story with a happy result because of your services. If your readers know you want such ideas, most won't hesitate to share them. Making these a regular feature will encourage even more leads that you can parlay into human interest stories.

- ❑ **Stay abreast of local and national news.** Perhaps your community has a wave of newly minted American citizens or has recovered from a plant closing and is back to full employment. Did your organization assist in those efforts to earn citizenship or find jobs? Look for some of the best examples illustrating your progressive partnerships for news articles.

- ❑ **Have a good hook.** Your organization delivers on its mission every day, so avoid pitching the routine for media coverage. Look to spotlight how that mission is changing lives. For example, when the child of the Sudanese family you have been helping earns a full academic scholarship to the university.

One-page Report Is a Must Read

Some organization's tend to think annual reports must be lengthy to convey their message. However, Julianne Kalasinski, communications coordinator, United Neighborhood Centers of Lackawanna County (Scranton, PA), says that is not always true and has done the opposite — created a one-page report.

She uses one 11 X 17-inch sheet of paper. Its size, colors and the quality of the photographs make it a must read.

"The annual report is printed in-house so I have complete control of its format," says Kalasinski. "Since the paper is larger than average, I use bigger pictures to attract my readers."

Kalasinski also uses a color scheme that matches the organization's logo color, which is dark maroon. She uses that color for the titles and subheads to link all the elements, making it easier on the eyes.

One sheet leaves no room for cluttering elements and eliminates flipping through pages.

"People think the report is shorter than average, so they are more likely to read it," Kalasinski says.

Source: Julianne Kalasinski, Communications Coordinator, United Neighborhood Centers of Lackawanna Country, Scranton, PA. Phone (570) 346-0759. E-mail: jkalasinski@unitedneighborhoodcenter.org

Increase Your Annual Report's Readership

An interesting and well-rounded annual report will appeal to a wider audience and promote readership, which leads to increased interest in your organization.

"We discovered using quotes and pictures from those who support the ministry augments the message," says Ellen Mitchell, vice president for donor and investor relations, Church Extension (Indianapolis, IN). In their last annual report, staff gave narratives of their congregation services, their efforts to cultivate mission-driven stewards, etc. This was well received, says Mitchell, because it evidenced the ministry as provided through staff efforts. "We also highlight an investor or donor so people can see how their investments and gifts help Church Extension live out its mission. In addition, we use attractive, full-color designs to grab attention," she says.

The report distribution process also has an effect on readership. Discover new ways to get your report to the public and consider your community's diversity and demographics when preparing and distributing your report. "We mail the reports, hand them out at general and regional assemblies and provide Spanish copies," Mitchell says. She carries, distributes and uses the annual report in her face-to-face visits with prospective supporters because it clearly outlines options for supporting the ministry. She also puts the report on their website as a PDF file.

Source: Ellen L. Mitchell, Vice President for Donor and Investor Relations, Church Extension, Indianapolis, IN. Phone (800) 274-1883. E-mail: emitchell@churchextension.org

Simplify Annual Report Figures

Keep your audience in mind when creating your organization's annual report.

While including some fiscal information is important, it is even more important to make this information easy for your readers to understand. This is not to say a Form 990 or portions of your audited financial statement cannot be included. However, adding a brief explanation can help readers interpret these reports.

Realizing that your financially savvy readers may be interested in more details and able to digest more complicated materials, offer information in your annual report on how to obtain a full copy of your auditor's report, either in hard-copy format or as an online link to a PDF document.

Community Report Reaches Far and Wide

Many nonprofits produce an annual report. While this can be an effective communications tool, there are other ways to illustrate your organization's achievements and goals.

Colleen Hart, communications manager — Foundation, Community Hospice of Northeast Florida, (Jacksonville, FL) explains. "As a community-based and community-supported nonprofit, we wanted a cost-effective way to report our fiscal year accomplishments to as many people in our service area as possible. Unfortunately, the narrow distribution and longer format of our traditional annual report was not adequately reaching and informing our audience. We began exploring different formats and costs and determined an eight-page insert in the local newspaper would reach the broad community we serve at a per unit cost that was 20 times less than the traditional annual report."

The hospice worked with the local newspaper's sales rep to schedule the insertion at a strategically beneficial time — the Friday before the opening of the organization's newest inpatient center. A total of 200,000 community reports were produced for insertion in the Florida Times Union (174,000 copies), its sister publication, the St. Augustine Record (21,000 copies); 5,000 copies were distributed to donors at the $1,000-plus giving level; and others were used as informational giveaways at health fairs, seminars and in the lobbies of the inpatient facilities.

Explore new ways of sharing traditional annual report information in more non-traditional ways.

"The process of creating our community report did not differ much in terms of the steps used for gathering the information. Instead of feature profiles on patients, staff, volunteers and supporters, we relied on photos and extended captions. Rather than a narrative explaining the past fiscal year's achievements, we used more graphics and charts to sum up our accomplishments and progress."

To give the community report a different look, it featured:

- An open letter from the organization's president and CEO, persuading readers to be proactive about exploring their end-of-life care options and rely on Community Hospice for support and resources.
- A main body divided in three themed sections based on the organization's position as a mission-driven, community-supported and community-based nonprofit.
- The past fiscal year's achievements and progress according to the appropriate theme (e.g., a community supported section showcasing volunteers and philanthropic contributions).

Source: Colleen Hart, Communications Manager — Foundation, Community Hospice of Northeast Florida, Jacksonville, FL. Phone (904) 407-6132. E-mail: chart@communityhospice.com

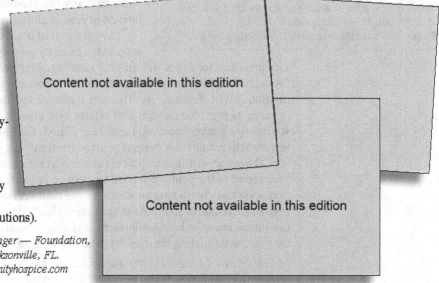

Content not available in this edition

Content not available in this edition

Offer Constituents a Quick Overview of Your Organization

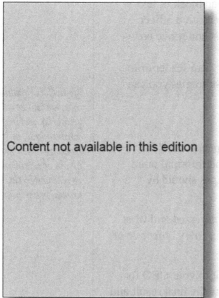

Content not available in this edition

Whether in an annual report, recruitment brochure or a PR piece, sharing a facts-at-a-glance section may be a quick and easy way to highlight your organization.

Michael Hartnett, director of marketing and research, Greater Baltimore Medical Center (Baltimore, MD), says the facts-at-a-glance page in an annual Discover publication is an excellent way to offer constituents a quick overview of the hospital.

"With time at a premium these days, a one-page summary is a great way to share the most important data with people in a way that is user friendly," says Hartnett.

The page presents common points of comparison for hospitals (e.g., number of beds, number of inpatient admissions, etc.); primary and secondary service areas; residence programs; a facilities overview; plus key statistics such as numbers of emergency room visits, births and average length of stay.

Information gathered for the facts-at-a -glance page is used throughout the year, Hartnett says, as a point of comparison for other hospitals, resource for journalists, in physician and executive recruitment, donor relations, and in presentations to board members/prospective board members and legislators.

Source: Michael Hartnett, Director of Marketing & Research, Greater Baltimore Medical Center, Baltimore, MD. Phone (443) 849-3881. E-mail: mhartnet@gbmc.org

Get Most Mileage Possible Out of Annual Reports

Annual reports can provide valuable insight into a nonprofit. But what do you do with your organization's annual reports besides send them to those persons on your mailing list?

Here are some additional uses:

1. Deliver copies to offices with a request that they be placed in the lobby for visitors.

2. Use extra copies to introduce your nonprofit to new prospects.

3. Have copies available for the taking at receptions both at home and away.

4. Include with letters of introduction or proposals to foundations/corporations.

5. Exchange with other nonprofits to garner ideas for next year's publication.

6. Ask board members and volunteers to share copies with friends/colleagues.

7. Distribute copies of the reports when making presentations to clubs and civic organizations.

Annual Report Tips

Get the facts right. The only thing worse than producing no annual list of contributors is producing one with incorrect information. Take extra pains to:

- Spell names correctly.
- Classify correctly according to amount contributed.
- Include (or not include) spouse as preferred by the donors.
- Credit matching company gifts.
- List donors names in all categories for which they qualify (e.g. alumni, memorials, endowed gifts, etc.).

Check and re-check correctness. The extra effort you take to get names listed and spelled correctly will minimize mistakes.

- Have multiple individuals review your list of contributors before it goes to print.
- Send a draft list of contributors to your constituency to confirm accuracy of information and garner additional gifts.
- When in doubt, pick up the phone and contact the donor for clarification.

Make Your CEO's Message Purposeful

Many annual reports published by charitable institutions contain a rarely read block of text on the inside cover or first page — a message from the president or chief executive officer. Most readers spot words like excellence and commitment, anticipate the rest and move on — especially when times are stable and there has been little bad news.

As a development officer, you may be asked to write such a message for your leader or to suggest content for a message he/she writes and asks you to edit. Here are strategies you can consider:

When you write the message:

- **Know how your CEO thinks and speaks.** Some of the most eloquent speakers feel uncomfortable with written communications. Is the CEO plain spoken and informal or an amateur actor who has played Hamlet with good reviews? Written messages should be consistent with speaking and personal style.

- **Do an interview before writing.** Ask your CEO what issues should be addressed and what he/she wants to say to readers — in order of importance. Emphasize the primary objective of the message — to thank, to convey achievements, to invite support, etc.

- **Prepare a draft for review.** Write the message as you see fit, then offer it to your CEO for approval. Ask that all changes be made quickly and returned to you. Show the final result and offer only one more opportunity for last-minute editing.

When you are the editor:

- **Your CEO may be an articulate writer.** Consider yourself lucky if his/her copy is clean and concise. But do offer a small list of suggestions that are of great current interest to your donors. In your position, you may be more attuned to issues or questions about which your constituency may wish to know.

- **Discuss the content of the rest of the publication.** If your annual report has a special theme and a common thread throughout each section, be sure the CEO is familiar enough with each so the message will complement other content.

- **If your CEO writes poorly but thinks he/she writes well, it is time for your diplomatic skills.** The message may be long and cumbersome. Tell him/her you have read it, but space will be tight — ask if he/she can shorten it. The second phase includes your own subtle editing (without changing the meaning of any phrase) by eliminating unnecessary words. Rearrange or combine sentences to enhance paragraph flow. When you resubmit it, the subtle changes may very well go unnoticed, or the improvements may be appreciated.

- **Ask first if your editing is acceptable before the message is written.** Communication is a key when the CEO actually expects you to clean it up, but you don't for fear of causing ill will. Talk about editing preferences at the first opportunity — if you haven't seen his/her writing before, you aren't being judgmental, but courteous. You simply want to know what is expected of you as editor of this and other publications.

- **Collect several CEO messages from other organizations.** Have a sampling of both good and poor examples to build your case for brevity. Send each to the CEO as an FYI with your succinct summary of each stack: "These were brief but meaty," or "Notice how many words these writers used to say nothing?" Add that you thought he/she might find them interesting or amusing.

- **Offer a list of words to use or avoid.** One major problem with CEO messages is overuse of cliché words such as dedication, excellence, commitment and teamwork. Even though each of those describes your organization, review your thesaurus for better, fresher choices. Encourage your CEO to find as many fitting, simpler replacements as possible. Such simplification leaves a more heartfelt impression and makes your CEO's message stand out.

Your CEO's annual report message can be an attention-grabbing and inspiring communiqué, or it can be the exact opposite. That's why plenty of attention should be directed to this opening annual report message.

Give Your Donor List the Prominence It Deserves

When the telephone book shows up on your doorstep, what's the first thing you do? Look to see if you are in it, right?

That same gut reaction drives your donors to look for their names when they receive a publication from your cause.

When publishing an annual list of contributors — often the centerpiece of an annual report — realize it for the important act of stewardship it is. Check and double-check the spelling of names, giving levels, correct listing of spouses and other details before going to press.

Also, when designing your showpiece publication, be sure to avoid these pitfalls that diminish the honor roll's importance:

✓ Burying your annual list of contributors within a regular publication.

✓ Making the print so small it can hardly be read.

✓ Not categorizing gifts by size — increasingly larger gifts should be given more prominence.

One last thought: If you include asterisks or other marks behind donor names to indicate a certain giving level or status (e.g., alumni; lifetime donor), include definitions of what the coding means on each page. Don't frustrate readers by making them search for the key.

Tips for Creating Donor Lists

To help build a habit of annual giving — as well as increased loyalty — don't simply list persons' names. Include the consecutive number of years a donor has contributed when you publish your annual honor roll of contributors.

Here's an example:

8 Mark Brown

1 Mr. and Mrs. Herman Goodenow

15 Susan Haegger

1 Kurt Trucking

Donors take pride in seeing that number grow next to their name, and this practice may help you encourage people to renew annual pledges.

Postcard Encourages Gift Giving for Donor Honor Roll

What steps do you take to keep your supporters informed and enthusiastic about ongoing gift opportunities?

Each spring, alumnae of Simmons College (Boston, MA) receive a 5 X 7-inch postcard that gives them a chance to make a gift and get their name included in their class's Honor Roll of Donors, a class fundraising letter.

The four-color process postcard, shown below, features current undergraduate students and a professor along with a header that says, "They Are The Simmons Fund:. At the bottom, it says, "Won't YOU Be Too? Make your gift by February 15th to be named in your class's Honor Roll of Donors".

Simmons personnel sent the postcard to 16,000 undergraduate alumnae who had not yet given in the fiscal year.

"The design of this piece is a continuation of our annual direct mail campaign messaging and brand," says Julianne Silva, associate director, The Simmons Fund.

"We began the Who is The Simmons Fund? You are The Simmons Fund! campaign in the 2006 fiscal year," Silva says. "The campaign included photos of our own students, faculty, staff and alumni and included a case for support of The Simmons Fund — the college's annual fund."

The back of the postcard directs alumnae to make their gift online, by phone or by mail. Alums who make gifts by mail are asked to include a specific tracking code on the check's memo line. The appeal code generated $11,383 in its first year.

While it's hard to measure the impact of this piece because many alumnae may not have included the tracking code with their gift, Silva believes the Honor Roll is an effective fundraising tool for The Simmons Fund.

Content not available in this edition

Source: Julianne Silva, Associate Director, The Simmons Fund, Simmons College, Boston, MA. Phone (617) 521-2342. E-mail: julianne.silva@simmons.edu

Nonprofit Publications What You Need to Know to Create Winning Publications

NEWSLETTER AND/OR MAGAZINE PRODUCTION

Whether you produce a newsletter or a magazine, whether it's distributed monthly or quarterly, whether it's sent through the mail or available online or both, it's important that any nonprofit organization, large or small, share regular written communications with the members of its extended family: those served by your organization, board members, donors, would-be donors, volunteers, community leaders, employees, members of the media and more.

Five Ways to Improve Your Printed Materials

Printed materials like newsletters, brochures, flyers and direct mail pieces are among the primary vehicles for showcasing your organization's image, so taking steps to ensure that they are as informative, effective and attractive as possible will help improve the results you hope to achieve from them.

1. **Develop a consistent look from piece to piece.** Consistency in graphics, typefaces, color and style helps your audience identify the materials as yours. This can be achieved partly by using ink colors that match your logo. If your logo is blue and black and your brochure is printed in two colors, use those colors even if basic design differs.
2. **Make it readable and uncluttered.** The first step in keeping a clean look for your project is editing content. Messages should be brief. Too much copy can mean too small a type size and make your design text-heavy. For easy readership, use at least 11-point type for plain text.
3. **Every photo should have meaning.** Photos should speak as clearly as your written word, showing people working for your organization. A picture of your building on the front of your brochure tells readers little. Use it instead next to a map of how to reach your facility where it can be a helpful; highlight people on the front.
4. **Choose sufficient paper stock weight.** Lighter weight stocks can save money, but sometimes don't hold up to rigors of mail delivery or distribution at events. Test stock samples from the printer first, cut to the size of your printed piece, and see if it will withstand crumpling.
5. **Pay attention to copy and art placement.** Remember that there's nothing wrong with some white space, you need not fill every inch of your publication. Keep copy, art or photos that are related to each other on the same page or panel when possible, or stay part of a design block. Avoid column and page jumps when you can.

Here are five basic principles to make your publications more informative, effective and attractive.

Develop Criteria to Evaluate Story Worthiness

How does your communications office identify possible feature stories? Do you have a procedure in place to determine if an idea is the right fit for your publications?

Jovi Craig, communications manager, International School of the Peninsula (Palo Alto, CA), says thoroughly evaluating an article's premise is a serious job.

"Stories are a snapshot and window into one's organization," says Craig, so make sure that opening is showing viewers the image and giving them the message you want them to receive.

Craig considers three criteria before pursuing a feature story:

1. **The story must be reflective of the organization's mission.** "One of my goals is to make sure each story ties into the mission of our school or into our school's educational philosophy. I think it's important someone who doesn't know our organization, after reading all the stories, will know exactly who we are and what is important to us."
2. **The story must be of interest to the audience.** "In writing any piece, you always want to analyze who your audience is and what types of stories engage them. In addition to facts, go beyond that and look for stories with a human factor."
3. **The story must compel and connect.** Craig says this criteria plays off point No. 2. "A feature story should delve into how what happened has moved someone or positively influenced them — these are the stories that have the most impact with our audience." When identifying feature stories, Craig keeps in mind a phrase that resonated with her at a workshop — people may not remember what you said, but they will remember how you made them feel.

How do you know if a particular topic is worthy of being a feature story? Here's one way to answer that question.

Source: Jovi Craig, Communications Manager, International School of the Peninsula, Palo Alto, CA.
Phone (650) 251-8520. E-mail: jovicraig@istp.org

Employ Journalistic Judgment to Determine What to Publish

"How do you determine newsletter or magazine content?"

"Our philosophy for determining content is based largely on our experience in journalism. The editor and I have written for several newspapers and weeklies in the past, and we bring that news judgment to our current work. For each story, we consider our readers first — will they learn something new, find a little inspiration, be entertained?

"We want to feature stories that highlight the accomplishments and experiences of alumni, faculty and students, that create a sense of connection for both the alumnus who might create an endowment some day and the prospective student who wants to see what a Flagler education might offer. To reach those people, we focus on finding a variety of compelling content that appeals to a broad audience. We offer everything from photo galleries to news briefs to in-depth features on current issues and research. We find that content by acting like reporters — asking questions of faculty and staff, staying in touch with students and alumni, and keeping an eye on campus events and issues that might spark an idea."

— Liz Daube, Media Specialist, Public Information, Flagler College (St. Augustine, FL)

Here are three professional opinions on how to determine your newsletter or magazine content.

"The feature stories usually focus on a theme, whether it is an academic department, co-curricular projects or campaign. Our editorial team — consisting of myself, our assistant director of PR who oversees media relations and print publications, and our vice president for college advancement — considers significant events, news items, student stories and program changes and/or success to determine the theme of upcoming issues. Once determined, various angles are considered to address the theme, including campus news stories, related alumni stories, informal interviews with professors and students connected to the theme, etc. Feature stories, usually one primary and two secondary, are confirmed and completed.

"Sometimes the theme comes from a new program or initiative we choose to advance, e.g., a new college vision for the next three to five years and related planning processes. My assistant director and I use this information to develop a proposal, which I then present to our VP for his feedback."

— Robyn Florian, Director of College Relations & Marketing, Greenville College (Greenville, IL)

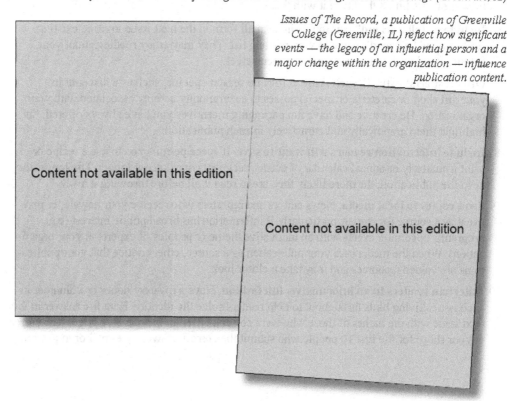

Issues of The Record, a publication of Greenville College (Greenville, IL) reflect how significant events — the legacy of an influential person and a major change within the organization — influence publication content.

Content not available in this edition

Content not available in this edition

10 Ways to Increase Your Publication's Readership

Assuming your organization's newsletter or magazine is being read, it serves many purposes: informing customers, supporters and volunteers of important progress being made, recognizing valued contributors and elevating your image of service and stewardship in its content.

In crafting your publications or reviewing them with a critical eye, remember that most supporters will read your publication much the same way they read a daily newspaper. Some will go first to the sports page, others to the stock market or lifestyle page. They may read every section, or skim their favorite pages. Special sections may be saved if they contain coupons, calendars or other information that will be useful in coming days.

How can you adapt some of the variety a daily newspaper offers into your organization's publications to increase readership? Here are 10 ways that may help:

1. **Use as many names as possible in stories**. Names are news, especially when they are easy to read with bold type for emphasis and woven into important information about your events or programs. This also helps recognize those who helped your cause in some way.

2. **Feature one or two short people profiles in each issue**. They need not be long and detailed — the shorter they are, the more you can use. Readers will begin to look forward to this addition. Use a small head-and-shoulders photo if possible.

3. **Invite readers to be contributors**. Find a variety of ways that allow readers to assist with content, such as asking them to offer their favorite time-management technique to share with others, or a few sentences about "the best volunteer job I ever had." Use all you can, and hold extras for the next issue.

4. **Print positive unsolicited input when appropriate**. When a donor sends a short note with a contribution (many do include a brief message), include it in a highlighted box on your contribution page if appropriate. Ask permission first, however. Readers will begin looking for regular messages after a few issues, or begin writing some of their own with their checks.

5. **Increase distribution**. Leave a few copies of your publication in the lobby, at the front desk, in the cafeteria, a lounge or coffee room. Waiting areas are especially attractive because people may be looking for something to do. Have enough of a stack available so they know it's fine if they take it with them.

6. **Include a "tell a friend" coupon**. Print a small form in the next issue inviting existing readers to add a friend's name to your mailing list. They may enjoy reading about your activities and wish to become involved themselves.

7. **Offer a special extra in each issue**. It may be season-specific, such as a discount in your gift shop or cafeteria or special passes to a community activity associated with your organization. Be creative and have fun packaging incentives you have always offered, but highlight them graphically and attractively in each publication.

8. **Include information readers will want to save**. If space permits you to use a recipe or print a quarterly or annual calendar of events, recipients may keep it longer. The longer they keep the publication, the more likely they are to read it all before throwing it away.

9. **Send copies to local media**. News editors and reporters who receive your newsletter may use it as a source for stories, particularly if information has broad public interest (e.g., programs, upcoming events with an innovative theme or profiles of experts in your organization). When the media uses your publication as a source, others notice that your publications are valued resources and may take a closer look.

10. **Entertain readers in an informative, fun fashion**. Have a mystery donor or volunteer in each issue, giving hints throughout to help readers solve the identity. Print the answer in the next issue with the names of those who were correct. Offer an inexpensive prize (free coffee at your shop) for the first 10 people who submit the correct answer by e-mail or in person.

The bottom line for any publication is to get it read, understood and, in many instances, move the reader to action. These 10 principles will help ensure that your publications get read.

Work Human Interest Stories Into Your Publications

Human-interest stories should have a place in your organization's publications.

Whether they tug at constituents' heartstrings, stir up a call to action or simply entertain, if chosen and written correctly they can leave a powerful impression among your audience.

So what does your organization do to keep these stories present in your publications?

Julia Brennan, director of communications, Kimball Union Academy (Meriden, NH), shares several techniques she employs to help her identify feature stories and share them with the media:

People like reading about other people. Here are some ways that officials with one academy works human interest stories into their publications.

- ❑ Meeting with the school's external affairs team (Brennan, assistant head of external affairs and head of school) to identify strategic priorities and initiatives that might guide editorial content.
- ❑ Attending all school, alumni and development meetings.
- ❑ Attending athletic events.
- ❑ Keeping her ears to the ground for news and events of interest to the academy's constituents.

Brennan says these simple but effective, techniques have led her to some great feature stories.

"I look for human interest stories that focus on the impact a Kimball Union education has had in preparing alums for various accomplishments.

"For example, we recently wrote an article on a 20-year-old alum who competed in Beijing in track," says Brennan. "I also look for interesting stories about our students, like a story that will be featured in an upcoming publication on two students who spent the summer bicycling across the U.S. to raise money for a school in Kenya."

Other features generated by Brennan's techniques include a story celebrating the 30th anniversary of the return to coeducation at the school featuring distinguished women alumnae from different decades; the opening of the school's new campus center and the transformational impact made by a $5 million gift.

Source: Julia Brennan, Director of Communications, Kimball Union Academy, Meriden, NH. Phone (603) 469-2332. E-mail: jbrennan@kua.org

Establish and Stick to Newsletter Deadlines

Which would people rather see — a letter-perfect newsletter that shows up in their mailbox or e-mail inbox once in a while, or a nearly perfect newsletter that arrives on a predictable basis?

Most would prefer the latter and would choose timeliness over perfection.

Getting the product to your supporters on a regular basis will reinforce your organization's image of being dependable, consistent and having longevity. But getting it to them sporadically — or sending your summer issue filled with family travel ideas in late August — could give the impression that your organization is disorganized, unstructured or just doesn't care about details.

Establish and stick to production deadlines for your publications. Keep in mind, readers will more readily forgive a typo or misspelling in an article about a special event than they would receiving a letter-perfect newsletter advertising the event —but having it show up three days after the event took place.

Tips to Decide Your Publication's Frequency

A newsletter can serve as a useful tool for your organization to spread important news and updates as a community resource, but how often should you publish editions of the newsletter?

"Two reasons why the decision was made to go with a quarterly version of our newsletter were cost and schedule," says Sharon Myers, director of communications, St. Joseph's Collegiate Institute (Buffalo, NY). "As a nonprofit we always need to keep an eye on the bottom line and putting out a full-color newsletter is a costly exercise so the quarterly option is more appealing to us. The second part of this equation is our schedule — the quarterly version follows the school schedule perfectly."

When deciding on your publication's frequency, consider the scope of information that will be included in each publication. "We tend not to focus on the day to day in our magazine, leaving that to the other facets of our marketing function — primarily through our website, as well as an e-mail newsletter that is sent to various constituencies depending on the message. This helps with timeliness and allows us to keep information current and flowing. The dates we include in the magazine have been set a year in advance so the likelihood of change is slim."

Source: Sharon Myers, Director of Communications, St. Joseph's Collegiate Institute, Buffalo, NY. Phone (716) 270-4119. E-mail: smyers@sjci.com

Keep Content Fresh When Producing Quarterly Publications

Keeping your publication content timely and newsworthy is important. However, for publications that come out only a few times a year — such as a quarterly newsletter — keeping content fresh can be tough.

"Keeping things fresh with a quarterly magazine is a challenge," says Mike Bruckner, vice president, public relations, Muhlenberg College (Allentown, PA). "With a magazine that only comes out four times a year, it's hard to give them something fresh, newsworthy and interesting, so you look for different angles or quirky pieces of information. Certain areas, such as sports, are even harder since the season might be over by the time the magazine comes out."

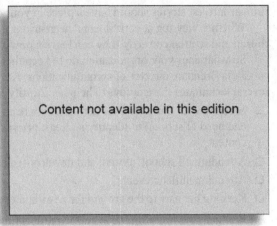

Content not available in this edition

A feature story on Juliusz Draganski, a Polish immigrant and 25-year employee of Conception Abbey (Conception, MO), is an example of a feature story perfect for a quarterly publication.

Look for Unusual News Angles

Faced with the timeliness issue of reporting on the football season in the quarterly publication, Muhlenberg Magazine, Bruckner and his colleagues took a different approach. Instead of recapping the season well after it had ended, they printed an article written by an alum who was also a former player on the college's football team.

"Our magazine editor is an alum and friends with the former football player," says Bruckner. "The two were talking about the season and how exciting it was. He started saying that he came to a few games, but as the season wore on, he got into it, and started explaining how he followed the game at home. She asked him if he would like to write about it.

"The story consisted of him talking about his time here; coming to homecoming and watching the team; and then watching the team beat our long-time rival and ultimately winning the season finale to go undefeated. He could not make every game, so he was on his computer and had the stats live on the computer with the broadcast of the game on the Web."

Provide Insight Into Your Organization's Unique Services, People

Staff at Conception Abbey and Seminary College (Conception, MO) take a similar approach to quarterly publications, says Jarrod Thome, director of communications.

"In our quarterly printed publication, the main articles are not always news stories per se, but often articles that give insight into different facets of our institution — the kinds of things you'd only know by living or working here," says Thome. "Maybe they'll highlight a lesser-known area or present a well-known one in a different light or through a different person's point of view."

Thome provides an example of a story featured in the winter issue of Tower of Topics magazine.

"I wrote an article on the 25 years of employment of Conception Abbey's painter. He is a Polish immigrant who came to the United States as a refugee during Communist rule of Poland. The article is about how he left his country, came to Conception Abbey, the life he found here, and why he's still happy to be here after 25 years. Not many people who know about Conception knew Juliusz Draganski's story; now they do, and with it, they know the effect that Conception Abbey can have on people."

By providing articles that highlight the unique culture or history of your organization, you will keep the content of your publication fresh and inviting.

Keeping content fresh for a quarterly pub can be challenging. Learn how these two organizations are tackling that issue.

Sources: Mike Bruckner, Vice President, Public Relations, Muhlenberg College, Allentown, PA. Phone (484) 664-3230. E-mail: bruckner@muhlenberg.edu. Website: www.muhlenberg.edu
Jarrod Thome, Director of Communications, Conception Abbey, Conception, MO.
Phone (660) 944-2823. E-mail: jthome@conception.edu. Website: www.conception.edu

Borrow Our Ideas: Modify NCR Ideas to Suit Your Needs

Kathy Auchey, director, fund development and public relations, Margaret E. Moul Home (York, PA), has borrowed many ideas from The Nonprofit Communications Report (NCR) to use in her own organization. In 2007, she combined two such ideas to develop a staff contest to rename the organization's newsletter.

"A little over a year ago I suggested we change the name of our newsletter and started a contest with the employees to come up with a new name," Auchey says. "When the recommendation was discussed with the committee about changes for our newsletter, I remembered reading an article in the NCR about involving employees in newsletter writing. Another article recommended staff contests for any naming needs for an organization, so we combined the two concepts.

"The home celebrated 25 years of service to its residents in 2007 and we wanted to revitalize the community awareness, reestablish a good relationship with the supporters and give the home a look of quality," she says. "With the help of the marketing professional from the board and my own marketing background, we enhanced the logo, and updated the colors and developed a tag line for the home. With all of these changes, we wanted the name of our quarterly newsletter to reflect our new look and let people know that it gave them information about the Margaret E. Moul Home."

Using concepts detailed in NCR, Auchey and her staff created a contest that suited their needs and produced winning results. "We attached an entry form to employees' pay envelopes, in addition to posting fliers all over the staff areas," she says. "Entries were very creative, clean and proper, and exactly what we were looking for."

Auchey says that she often finds herself borrowing from several ideas to create a completely new concept: "NCR has helped me in so many ways — suggestions for press releases, redesigning our brochures to be more informative, PR for special events, and our quarterly newsletter, just to name a few. If NCR doesn't offer a specific idea to use, it will generate an idea for our communications needs for other situations."

Source: Kathy M. Auchey, Director Fund Development & Public Relations, Margaret E. Moul Home, York, PA. Phone (717) 767-6463, ext. 138. Website: www.margaretemoul.org

Simple Newsletter Brings Success

Don't underestimate the power of a simple communication piece.

Arizona State University's monthly newsletter, News You Need to Know (NYNTK), has been a successful communication tool for 13 years.

"Except for its earliest days when the newsletter was trying to find its legs, the format has stayed the same — a one side, self-mailer," says Wilma Mathews, director of constituent relations. "In reader surveys, exactly half request more items be put on the back side and exactly half want to leave it the way it is. We opt for the latter."

Reader surveys indicate the most important factor to its success is the newsletter's brevity. "I can get in six to nine items monthly, which keeps the readers happy because there are items to choose from," Mathews says.

Mathews searches the university for news items — individual achievements, which must be national or international in scope, as well as new offerings, student accomplishments, research updates and significant gifts.

A successful newsletter benefits the entire organization. NYNTK is targeted to people of influence, Mathews says. Other subscribers include key donors, alumni leaders and presidents of peer institutions. This range of readers means the mailing list is constantly changing and being updated.

"Keeping those in leadership in the know about ASU helps prevent the mystique that can accompany a large university such as ours," Mathews says. "It also constantly reinforces our key messages of quality and access."

Source: Wilma Mathews, Director of Constituent Relations, Arizona State University, Tempe, AZ. Phone (480) 727-6031. E-mail: wkm23@asu.edu

Get a continuous flow of great communications, PR, publications and marketing ideas from the monthly newsletter, Nonprofit Communications Report. To subscribe, go to www.stevensoninc.com

Do you publish an insider's newsletter for key donors, board members and others? Here's how one university addresses that issue.

Organization Keeps Newsletter Simple

Improve internal communications by sharing information in a format that is desirable to staff.

"What we've found works best is sending messages in advance, often and in many formats. Also, typically, we try to be as informal as possible, making information easy to pick up and put down at a moment's notice. In healthcare, especially in the clinical setting, our employees don't have a lot of time to catch up on internal affairs. We make points easy to access, easy to read and easy to pick back up if the reader is interrupted," says Bethany Berscheid, corporate marketing and communications coordinator, Deaconess Associations, Inc. (Cincinnati, OH).

Finding a balance that works for all departments and staff members can be tricky. "A few years ago, we had a quarterly, commercially produced color-formatted newsletter, called Pulse that went to all employees. It was a very professional piece, but it didn't engage our employees. We moved to a smaller, less dense version on a biweekly basis, but still employees didn't pick it up," says Berscheid. "Surprisingly, they've reacted best to a biweekly, colored paper, photocopied newssheet, Monday Letter, filled with short, snappy articles of need-to-know information. We found that formal messages just didn't get the message across. It was too intimidating and time consuming. Our employees needed something they could catch on the fly.

"The newssheet is produced every other Monday and is distributed by interoffice mail, posted in the employee portal of our hospital's website and displayed in well-traveled areas. We always include a message from our COO, a listing of employees who have won awards, news to know about such as changes in parking, benefits or department contact information, special event information and new hires."

Content not available in this edition

Source: Bethany Berscheid, Corporate Marketing and Communications Coordinator, Deaconess Associations, Inc., Cincinnati, OH. Phone (513) 559-2856. E-mail: bberscheid@nuvox.net

Draw Publication Interest With Entertaining Word Game

A word game or similar purely-for-fun feature just may increase readership of your newsletter or magazine.

The Research Leader, the bimonthly newsletter for the University of Dayton Research Institute (Dayton, OH), features either a word game or math-, logic- or visual-based brainteaser.

"If you pick up the newsletter to solve the puzzle, you might be more inclined to scan through the rest of the newsletter," says Pamela Gregg, communication administrator.

"Our readership within the research institute is as diverse as our employee population, which includes scientists, engineers, technicians and administrative staff," she says. "The same holds true for readers within our university setting but outside of the research institute. Because of this, we try to vary the type and difficulty level of the teaser."

Readers are asked to send in their answers, which gives Gregg an idea of who is reading the newsletter and allows her to tweak the content that would most interest her audience. Gregg says she receives 10 to 20 replies per game.

Source: Pamela Gregg, Communication Administrator, University of Dayton Research Institute, Dayton, OH. Phone (937) 229-3268. E-mail: pamela.gregg@udri.udayton.edu

Extreme Makeover, Publication Edition

To re-energize your communications efforts and better express your organization's messages, consider subjecting one of your publications to an extreme makeover.

"We did a complete overhaul of our Mount Mercy Magazine, which is published three times per year and hits approximately 60,000 households," says Molly G. Altorfer, director of communications and marketing, Mount Mercy College (Cedar Rapids, IA).

"One thing that catapulted the overhaul was the hiring of a new president," says Altorfer. "We wanted a fresh look to better capture the new and exciting initiatives that this president was bringing to Mount Mercy. In some ways we knew early on that we needed to revitalize the magazine so we could better tell his story and the college's."

Mount Mercy staff sent requests for proposal to several design firms. Once the proposals came back, a group of campus and community constituents was gathered to review the RFPs and meet with the designers. The firms were asked to explain their design concepts and answer questions from the group.

Sometimes it makes good sense to do a complete overhaul of your organization's publications.

"We hired a new designer, Benson & Hepker Design, a firm that is well-known in Iowa for their magazine design and production," says Altorfer. Staff met with the design firm in person and communicated via phone and e-mail throughout the project.

Goals they set out for the newly renovated publication included:

✓ To have a cleaner, more sleek design.

✓ To focus more on photos and improve use of photography in the design, steering away from the publication's more whimsical art design.

✓ To create a design that allowed for and complements more substantial articles.

The re-designed publication now includes more detailed and lengthy written features, more alumni success stories and more where-are-they-now features.

"We increased our photography budget (by at least $20,000) because we wanted to rely more heavily on strong photos rather than art cover designs," says Altorfer. "The costs of printing did not rise dramatically and the design team is very reasonable because they cater to non-profits and higher education, and truly have a love of doing magazines that are affordable for small private colleges."

The feedback to the re-designed publication has been extremely positive, she says.

"Faculty and staff find the magazine more relevant to them, even though our focus was a renewed connection with alumni," she says. "Additionally, we are actually receiving letters to the editors for the first time."

Interview design firms to find the one that is the best fit for your publication makeover, she says, noting: "It is imperative that your work styles and personalities match."

Source: Molly G. Altorfer, Director of Communications and Marketing, Mount Mercy College, Cedar Rapids, IA. Phone (800) 248-4504.

The newly designed magazine for Mount Mercy College relies heavily on strong photos and substantial articles.

Content not available in this edition

Content not available in this edition

Editor's Note Connects With Readers

Looking for new ways to connect with readers? Include an editor's note in your publications.

"Our readers are alumni, grateful clients and donors and we try to offer something for each in every issue. But the editor's note is a way to talk to them all and tie everything together," says Gail Luciani, director of communications, University of Pennsylvania School of Veterinary Medicine (Philadelphia, PA).

An editor's note is a great opportunity for you to express a personal sentiment to your readers and include information that may not fit elsewhere in your publication. "Because we feature different areas once each year, the editor's note is the perfect way to introduce the main topic and tie in the latest information on our website."

Depending on your publication's subject matter, you could utilize the editor's note in various ways. You can use this section to address a serious issue that has affected your organization, introduce an exciting new fundraising campaign or simply thank your members and volunteers for their dedication and support.

Source: Gail Luciani, Director of Communications, University of Pennsylvania School of Veterinary Medicine, Philadelphia, PA. Phone (215) 898-1475. E-mail: luciani@vet.upenn.edu

External Publications Advice

- When preparing content for newsletters or magazines intended for those on your mailing list, be sure the content is selected for external rather than internal audiences. It's sometime easy to be pulled to the wants and desires of employees who think their ideas should take precedence over other topics.

Streamline Your Newsletter Preparation

Finding ways to streamline the creation of your newsletter or other publications will save your staff valuable time. Teddie Burnett Sleight, media relations/communications, EASTCONN (Hampton, CT), shares strategies for successful newsletter production:

1. "Our executive director always takes the time to help plan the newsletter's content, a critical element in the newsletter's relevance and success," Sleight says. "During these planning sessions, the executive director, communications director and newsletter editor brainstorm story ideas."

2. Choose stories that market your programs and services, but focus on the stories with a timely news angle.

3. "We have a general newsletter template so everyone, including the readers, has a sense of what to expect, from the layout process through the finished product," says Sleight. "We place regular features, like our agency's workshop calendar or the table of contents, on the same pages for each issue."

4. Use larger pictures to move readers through the newsletter. Action photos or colorful head shots are a good choice. Always write captions for photos.

5. Have others read the issue, look for typos and offer feedback before it goes to press.

6. "We seek to cover stories that are actually newsworthy — innovative, new programs or services that will help educators in our districts, or state programs that will have an impact on our education region," says Sleight.

Source: Teddie Burnett Sleight, Media Relations/Communications, EASTCONN, Hampton, CT. Phone (860) 455-0707 ext. 3337. E-mail: tsleight@eastconn.org

Newsletter, Magazine Production Tip

- Make 2010 your most organized year yet! Here's a great way to start: Keep stand-up file folders on your desk for each of the newsletters or magazines you produce throughout the year. When an idea comes up or a story or photo is turned in for an upcoming issue, you can place it in the appropriate file and forget about it until it's time to generate a story list for the next issue.

Audience Lends Clue to Newsletter Length

Q. What is the right length for a print newsletter? How is that best determined?

"The right length for a nonprofit print newsletter is best determined by its printing cycle and the demographics of the publication's target audience. LifeGift (Houston, TX) prints quarterly newsletters that are six to eight pages in length.

How many pages should make up your print newsletter?

"Monthly publications should be shorter in length, while bi-annual prints could be longer. Most importantly, length should be determined by the demographic of the publication's target audience. For example, the length of publications targeting medical professionals should take into consideration the limited amount of free time that clinical staff has to read. Keep the content short but valuable."

— *Ariana Montelongo, PR and Minority Outreach Coordinator, LifeGift (Houston, TX)*

Print Newsletters Still Serve a Purpose

With new technology options for communication growing exponentially, do print newsletters still serve a purpose?

"Prints are the best for communicating high-value information that is expected to remain constant for long periods of time."

Yes, says Ariana Montelongo, PR and minority outreach coordinator, LifeGift (Houston, TX), a not-for-profit organ procurement organization that recovers organs and tissue for persons needing transplants in 109 Texas counties in north, southeast and west Texas.

"Prints are the best for communicating high-value information that is expected to remain constant for long periods of time (e.g., quarterly or annual financial reports, announcements of new leadership, etc.)," Montelongo says. "Thus, the hard copy still matters because it serves as a tangible resource of valuable information."

A print newsletter can also represent your organization's quality standards, provide legitimacy and let your constituents know that you care.

"Our quarterly newsletter is printed in full color on glossy paper with high-resolution images and a color scheme that matches our branding standards," she says. "Our newsletter recipients know that we care about them as an audience by judging the high quality (of both content and image) of the newsletter."

Perhaps most importantly, she says, is that, in spite of technology, some people will always prefer the printed form of communication, and the mission of communication initiatives is to reach all target audiences.

Source: Ariana Montelongo, PR and Minority Outreach Coordinator, LifeGift, Houston, TX. Phone (713) 349-2572. E-mail: Amontelongo@lifegift.org

Three Ways to Make Sure Your Publication Gets Read

You regularly mail or e-mail a newsletter about your organization, but how do you know if anyone actually reads it? To increase readability, keep these points in mind:

Here are three tips to help ensure your publications get read by those who receive them.

1. **Who is writing the newsletter?** Don't force the newsletter job on someone who doesn't want it. If the person writing the stories doesn't enjoy the process or possess talents to do so, your readers won't enjoy reading newsletter content.
2. **But we always do it that way!** If your newsletter is formatted identically issue after issue, your readers may toss it out of sheer boredom. Consider a publication makeover. While being true to your organization's mission is important, get creative with content, photos, graphics and other design elements to keep readers' attention.
3. **Give them something of value.** Reward people for reading your newsletter with a coupon, chance for discount tickets to an event or small token from your agency.

Source: John Minges, Non-Profit Consultant, Minges & Associates LLC, Greenville, NC. Phone (252) 758-9800. E-mail: john@minges.com

Guest Writers Invigorate Publications

To enliven your publications, create a guest column that allows qualified community members to write about a topic relating to your organization.

Depending on your publication's size and format, you may wish to invite community members to write an opinion piece or serve as reporters to research a story you are currently pursuing. Doing so is a great way to engage the community in your work and add a fresh element to your publications.

Community members will enjoy seeing their names in print. Plus, this concept lets you experiment with local writers. You never know, you may find a new staff writer in the process.

Possible topics for guest writers:

- Have the guest writer attend one of your events and write a review of it.

- Have the guest writer research a legislative issue affecting your organization — this could include interviewing local government officials on the subject.

- Ask one of your volunteers to serve as a guest writer and document his/her experience working with your organization.

Do you ever turn to guest writers? That can be a great way to add life to a publication.

Three Ways to Make People Care About the Bricks and Mortar

How do you get people to read about your construction projects, let alone care? Try one of these story angles to add interest to construction-related stories and in internal publications and pitch ideas to external media:

❑ **Focus on unique design elements.** The U.S. Marshal's Service Museum (Fort Smith, AR) will be housed under the five points of a stylized star representing a marshal's badge. The museum will include a 40-foot glass wall featuring a prominent view of the Arkansas River and a hall of honor, where small memorial stars representing the more than 200 marshals who died in the line of duty will shine down onto a reflective pool. These points of interest were included in a story about designing and funding the museum in the Arkansas Democrat Gazette.

❑ **Focus on staff support and involvement.** An article in Crain's Cleveland Business highlighted the fact that the foundation and staff of the Lakewood Hospital (Lakewood, OH) had pledged $5.5 million to help support a planned renovation.

❑ **Focus on staff opinions and reflections.** The Dallas Morning News profiled seven leaders of the resident companies of the Dallas Center for the Performing Arts (Dallas, TX), along with their hopes for the new center. They also included photos of the leaders at the construction site.

Technology-driven Campaign Boosts

Need more ideas to keep your construction project top of mind among donors, clients and the news media? Check out these technology-driven ideas:

✓ **Web logs.** Set one up to run for the life of the campaign. Feature entries by one key person such as the campaign chair, or offer a variety of perspectives from your CEO, development staff, construction head, lead donor, etc.

✓ **E-newsletters.** Send monthly or quarterly updates to keep the project top of mind for prospective and invested donors.

✓ **Webcams.** Focus yours on the construction site to let folks track progress online.

✓ **Social networking sites.** Start a fan page through Facebook (www.facebook.com) or keep supporters updated through Twitter (www.twitter.com). Include photo updates.

✓ **Online video.** Take video at various key points in the campaign and post to your website or on sites such as YouTube (www.youtube.com).

Do you sometimes find it challenging to write about facilities or equipment? Here are some tried-and-tested ways of making those topics more palatable to readers.

Magazine Revamp Boosts Magazine's Features, Interest

Get more mileage out of your publications by giving them a makeover.

Kara Kane, director of communications, Medaille College (Buffalo, NY) says that since revamping their alumni magazine, college officials have received overwhelmingly positive responses, with the majority of those surveyed rating the writing and design as good to excellent. The undergraduate admissions office even ordered a second run to distribute to prospective students and parents.

Kane cites a few of the factors contributing to the design's success:

✓ They brought the magazine design in-house, saving money and time, since the design will be used as a template for future issues.

✓ Alumni, staff and current students contributed photos and feature content, and assisted with editing and proofreading.

✓ Each issue focuses on a specific theme. The premiere issue focused on Medaille being Buffalo's college, emphasizing stories on alumni who contributed to the city of Buffalo.

✓ The new design incorporates popular magazine features giving it a professional look and feel. Photos are made more artistic with knockouts and large pictures. Pull-out quotes, fact/statistic boxes and graphic images/number facts are also used.

✓ The magazine is published to the Web as well (issuu.com/medaille), opening up the audience to alumni and friends of the college who may have opted not to receive mail.

The magazine is now a twice-yearly publication that goes to nearly 14,000 people. The time and effort spent on the revamp was totally worth it, Kane says, but cautions people to take the appropriate amount of time for planning in order to deliver a quality piece. "With enough good ideas and subjects," she says, "the stories will write themselves!"

Source: Kara Kane, Director of Communications, Medaille College, Buffalo, NY. Phone (716) 880-2884. E-mail: kara.m.kane@medaille.edu

Focus on Publicizing Gifts' Impact

Never miss an opportunity to publicize how gifts to your nonprofit positively impact your organization and those you serve. Doing so encourages similar gifts.

Consider these examples as you prepare future gift-related publicity:

• **New equipment** — Instead of focusing only on the gift or giver, talk about ways this new equipment helps you better serve your constituents. Be prepared to point out how the equipment improves your position against the competition.

• **Named endowment funds** — Rather than dwelling on the donor alone, emphasize the ways annual interest from this gift will make a difference in the lives of those you serve. Point out how the program's future will be ensured for generations since the fund's principal will always remain intact.

• **New or enhanced programs** — Focus on the ways the new services provided will better serve your customers and the community or region at large. Profile one individual who benefits from the gift, or focus on the collective benefits of the new or improved program.

Besides helping to plant seeds in the minds of would-be donors, your stories' emphasis on the gifts' accomplishments will provide more interesting reading and consequently be remembered longer than if you focus on the gift or giver alone.

When was the last time you gave your publications a makeover?

It's wise to get as much publicity as possible about the gifts and grants your organization receives. Doing so helps to encourage others to make similar gifts and provides deserved recognition to the donors.

Nonprofit Publications What You Need to Know to Create Winning Publications

WRITING AND EDITING: COPY, CONTENT AND PROOFING

Bottom line: The messages that your publications convey really matter. What you choose to say and how you say it will hopefully move the reader to act in some way. Your publications and their contents convey the collective personality of your organization. They should share the heart and soul of what you're all about. That's why it's so important to give your copy the time and thought that it deserves.

Writing Advice

To make your copy more compelling, recognize that you are the seller and your reader is the buyer.

You can't force someone to buy a product or service or program; the reader has to want it. So before you begin writing, list your primary objective at the top of the document: "To convince more area residents that they will get the best available care by choosing our hospital."

Brochure Writing Advice

About to write copy for a new brochure? Remember these key points:

- When preparing your brochure's text, always remember that brevity counts. Create graphic elements and use text creatively to help the reader grasp key points by simply glancing through the piece.

- Speak directly to the potential customer, donor or volunteer: "We help you..."

- Use headings and subheadings to group like ideas and help readers focus on items that are of greatest interest to them.

Writing Tips

Just do it. Rather than waste time waiting for the "write" moment, it's easier to just start writing and see where it takes you.

Five Ways to Identify Story Ideas

It's not enough to simply produce and pitch story ideas to the media. Yours need to stand out among the crowd of other nonprofits. Here are five ways do that:

1. **Point out what makes you unique.** Ask yourself what are we doing that's different? Ask others in your organization, too. Their unique insight may bring up an aspect of your services that is due for time in the spotlight.

2. **Tie into the season.** Make a story out of how your organization's work is relevant to the time of year. In winter, have your resident health expert address how to avoid colds and flu. In summer, advertise that your classes are in air-conditioned comfort. In fall, feature how volunteering helps overcome empty-nest syndrome. And in spring, invite media as your clients and volunteers plant a garden together.

3. **Point out changes in how you do things, and why.** Are you offering more episodic volunteer opportunities? Providing more weekend services? Expanding on a program due to community need? Use the change to showcase your services.

4. **Consider talking about problems facing your organization.** Are budget problems forcing you to consider program cuts? Does pending legislation threaten your organization in some way? Consider the value of bringing to the public's attention those challenges your organization or industry is facing.

5. **Ride on the shirttail of local, regional, national or international news.** Reporters are always looking for fresh, local angles on current issues. Tie what's in the news with the services you provide or have experts offer a local perspective. Spotlight what you're doing to help, such as collecting personal hygiene items for tsunami survivors or offering emergency shelter to persons displaced by area wildfires.

In a rut when it comes to story possibilities? Check out these five ideas.

Crafting Then-and-now Stories for Maximum Effect

Then-and-now stories can show longevity, stability and growth.

In addition, staff with the Make-A-Wish Foundation of Northeast New York (Cohoes, NY) learned, comparing where your organization (or a client or a staff person or a program) has been and where it is today can clarify your mission.

Dogged by the misperception that all the children Make-A-Wish serves are terminally ill, the communications staff decided then-and-now stories were the perfect way to show that persons who had their wishes granted 10, 15 or even 20 years ago were still alive and thriving.

The concept was a huge success, with more than 20 former wish children acting as ambassadors at events and appearing in feature stories in media outlets throughout the foundation's territory.

The following tips were used by foundation staff to ensure the effort met with success:

☐ **Start early.** This gives you time to follow up with as many respondents as possible, guaranteeing the most compelling stories. You may also need time to locate certain people who have lost contact over the years.

☐ **Have a point.** Create a theme to tie stories together and drive a certain message home. Maybe your hospital is about to install leading-edge research equipment and you're planning a capital campaign. Showing donors how far you have come can encourage them to invest in how far you can go.

☐ **Flesh out subjects.** Allow potential subjects to talk about who they are now as a whole, not just in relation to your organization. Doing so will help you target additional media outlets.

☐ **Make the numbers.** If planning a major media or fundraising campaign based on then-and-now stories, make sure you have enough stories to keep the campaign fresh. Editors want new information, or at the very least, a new angle. Using the same story over and over again in your own publications can also turn people off.

☐ **Get the picture.** Include visual images from the past and today with any pitch for a then-and-now story.

Consider then-and-now stories to convey the strength and longevity of your organization.

Think Evergreen Stories

Just as an evergreen tree is in season and always fresh year-round, so is an evergreen story.

Develop a half dozen evergreen articles or timeless story ideas about your organization. That way, when the news media calls for a quick story idea, or you come up with an empty column in your newsletter, you'll be ready.

Evergreen stories don't usually feature lots of statistics or hang on the news hook of a current event, pending legislation or board vote. They instead talk about ongoing programs or services; timeless subjects such as how your agency helps solve a societal problem; or general features such as volunteering or joining a planned gift giving club.

Here are 10 examples of possible evergreen stories to get you started:

1. Giving clubs and their benefits.
2. A day in the life of your organization.
3. Preparing for baby boomer retirees.
4. Volunteers' many invaluable roles.
5. Five ways your organization makes a positive difference in the community.
6. Ways to support your cause.
7. New options in volunteering (how today's busy people can still help).
8. Feature story on longtime volunteer.
9. Listing of your resident experts and topics on which they speak.
10. How to nurture philanthropy (focus on a family with an intergenerational history of supporting your cause).

Story Identification Idea

■ Piggyback on a holiday. Take a look at upcoming holidays. In what ways can you connect the work of your organization to the holiday? Come up with several ideas, complete with contact persons, and get on the phone to news directors for your local TV stations and the assignment editor for your local paper.

Create Catchy Titles to Draw Readers Into Stories

If you oversee production and editing of your organization's monthly newsletters, quarterly magazines and press releases, you already know the importance of eye-catching headlines to draw readers into your subject matter.

A headline such as Accounting's Beverly Johnson Named Employee of the Year, while serviceable, may be interesting only to people who already know her. Give the headline a little extra thought, though, and you'll draw more people into the story.

For example, a shorter headline can tell more about a person and also serve as a theme for the entire profile, a teaser on the cover and graphic element for the page spread. Give the reader at a glance an idea of the story to follow:

- **Use headline kickers for details**. A kicker is an informative line in a smaller font size above the main headline that adds information to the headline.

- **Connect accomplishments and hobbies**. If, for instance, you're profiling a board member noted for writing articles for professional journals and who never misses the annual summer motorcycle trek to Sturgis, SD, combine the diverse interests in a single title, Easy Writer. Another example, your payroll head repairs toys and sews doll clothes in her spare time to donate to charities. Carry the theme of how she's a Living Doll for the title and story of your article.

- **Make headline writing a staff activity**. Many magazines and publications have staff meetings to discuss editorial content prior to publication of each issue. Use such a meeting to outline the highlights of each article and brainstorm for the best headline. Encourage participants to say the first things that come to mind and play off each other to refine the results.

- **Is your subject quotable**? If the subject of your story is known for a certain phrase like "Yes, Dear" every few sentences during an open telephone conversation with his wife, or "Right away!" after every request for action, think of ways to incorporate them into your story and tie it to an overall theme and headline.

- **Borrow from literature and pop culture**. An article about your upcoming annual campaign with record high financial goals might be titled Great Expectations. Does the person's name evoke a popular title? For example, the vice president of purchasing, Jim Smith has returned from the vacation he spent helping Hurricane Katrina victims. A story about his trip might be titled Mr. Smith Goes to Gulfport.

Eye-catching headlines help to draw readers into your stories and brochure copy.

Overcome Writer's Block

Struggling with how to begin that next news release or brochure? Searching for the right words to craft that million-dollar proposal? Overcome your writer's block by following some of these tips:

- Forget perfectionism. Just write. You can go back and polish later.
- Think like a kid. Make it fun. If you don't like it, don't use it.
- Write continuously for 20 minutes. Don't worry about sentence structure or sequence. Just get your thoughts on paper and see where they take you.
- Avoid waiting until the deadline date. Doing so creates a sense of panic and hinders free thinking.
- Get away from it for a few minutes. Take a walk. Listen to some music. You'll find that a quiet break — uninterrupted by others — will allow ideas to surface on their own.
- Brainstorm. Write down whatever comes to mind on the topic you have chosen. Begin at the end. Begin at the middle. Rearrange the pieces later.
- Be prepared to write rubbish before you write the good stuff.

Anyone can succumb to writer's block from time to time. Here's how to shake it off and get back into your groove.

Although writer's block occurs even among more experienced writers, knowing how to work through it will help you.

User-friendly Stats Help Communicate Key Messages

When striving to create memorable materials, include meaningful information that entices readers. Catch eyes on an important point by illustrating statistical information.

Jennifer Muhm, vice president of public affairs, Washington Health Foundation (Seattle, WA), says, "Statistics have been vital to our organization's ability to communicate our message. Building an education and engagement campaign around data, we have cited statistics in brochures, newsletters, letters to lawmakers and on our website. It also allows readers to understand our organization's vision, as well as our position on policy issues."

Statistics can be a powerful tool in copy when used appropriately.

It's important to keep the information up to date, but you can highlight it in several formats without having to constantly change it. "Repeating the same statistics has also been effective in creating a sticky message for our campaign. For example, the release of the UHF state health rankings each December has provided us an opportunity to remind the media, our partner organizations, policymakers and the public of those areas in which Washington must improve," Muhm says.

Use statistics you feel will be powerful to the reader. Take time to gather compelling statistical information that will grab your audience's attention in a new way. "It's important that the statistics used by nonprofits can be buttressed by real cases or stories to give the statistics meaning. Reliable sources (e.g., government agencies, research institutes, colleges and universities and state or national commissions) will lend your facts credibility. As a nonprofit that works with a wide audience, it's often best to choose one or two major statistics around which to frame an article or message — using too many statistics will overwhelm readers and the main messages may get lost," Muhm says. "Repeat key statistics often."

Source: Jennifer Muhm, Vice President of Public Affairs, Washington Health Foundation, Seattle, WA. Phone (206) 577-1806. E-mail: JenniferM@whf.org

Three Useful Writing and Layout Tips

Any writer would benefit from these three common sense tips.

1. **Never write anything you wouldn't want your mother to read.** Avoid keying text into the rough draft you wouldn't want in the final. Be cautious with temporary space fillers such as blah blah blah or other nonsensical text. But as irritating as it is to find you forgot to replace this gobbledygook, it's infinitely more painful to see your finished newsletter with the sentence:

   "Make up interesting quote here for CEO to say," said CEO John Smith at the dedication ceremony.

2. **Don't copy and paste for style.** It may be easy to copy a headline or cutline from page 2 and paste it onto page 3 to get the proper type size and format. Don't. It's too easy to fail to replace them, resulting in confusion for your readers. Instead, establish a style palette and build fresh text blocks from there.

3. **Edit onscreen and on paper.** Use your computer program's spellcheck and other text editing functions to help identify typos, but don't assume if it looks good on your monitor, it's good to go. Always print a hard copy and do a final read-through on paper so you see what your readers will see.

Think That Publication Is Good to Go? Think Again

Some typos can be tricky. When proofing that annual report, major news release or other document that will be read by thousands, take extra precautions to make sure it's as close to letter-perfect as possible. It's easy to overlook:

- Duplicate words that that appear in a sentence.
- A typo in your phone number or website address.
- Incorrect versions of words such as its and it's, affect and effect, or a sentence that reads "Its good too know there all on bored."

A New Look May Help Proofreading

Editing and proofreading your own work can be a challenge, but you can make it a bit easier with a tip from The Writing Center at the University of North Carolina at Chapel Hill (Chapel Hill, NC).

Give your grant narrative, appeal letter, brochure or newsletter a new look — just for the purpose of copy editing. By simply adjusting the look of a document, you may be able to fool your mind into thinking it is a new document, and you'll read it in a fresh way that will help you identify typos and increase readability.

Try this by changing font size, color or type. Altering the document's spacing may help as well. Just remember — unless you want the changes to become permanent — to save the proof-only document as just that, Summer2009newsletter-prooftojudy.doc

Reduce Proofreading Scribbles

Want to reduce proofreading scribbles on your newsletter drafts? Tell your proofreaders you follow Associated Press (AP) style.

AP style does not capitalize titles, spell out longer months when giving a certain date, use postal state abbreviations and more.

When people know you're following a professional stylebook, they reduce useless red ink and grumbling.

Look Back to Catch Typos

Want a surefire way for catching spelling errors? Read your document backwards.

When you read the same document over and over again, it is easy to glance over certain words whether they are spelled correctly or not. Turning that around and reading from back to front, right to left allows you to look at each word individually, making it much easier to catch words that are misspelled.

Editing That Final Proof

You're holding the final proof of your major publication. With a signature from you, it hits the presses. Ideally, you'll have a day and several sets of eyes to check it over. But if you're under deadline pressure, or you're a one-person shop, before signing that OK to Print sheet, remember to:

- Find a quiet place where you can give the proof your full attention.
- Double-check every date, time, page number, phone number, website and street address.
- Take a ruler or straight edge and literally run down text columns, line by line, searching for typos.
- Eyeball the photos for color quality and cropping, and accompanying captions for correct information.
- Talk to the printer about anything in the proof that concerns you.

If major changes are needed, ask for another final proof before going to press. If doing so is cost-prohibitive, ask to watch over the designer's shoulder and OK final text/layout changes onscreen as they are made. Ask for a final copy to be printed on a less-expensive laser printer to take with you, or a full-color PDF to be e-mailed to you.

Proofreading Tips

- Proofread at least once aloud to hear the difference between what you meant to write and what you actually wrote.

- Place a ruler under each line as you read to give your eyes a manageable amount of text to read.

- Proofread for one type of error at a time. For instance, if you commonly struggle with comma placement, read through your draft once to find and fix any comma mistakes.

Double-check Typed URLs, Phone Numbers

One slip of the pinkie can send readers of your important publications in the wrong direction — sometimes with embarrassing consequences.

Take extra care to input telephone numbers, e-mail addresses and websites correctly the first time. When editing articles or publications, don't assume phone numbers, Web addresses, street addresses and other crucial contact information are correct. Actually read them for accuracy.

For phone numbers with which you are unfamiliar, pick up your phone and check them.

For websites, type them in and see if you have it correct. Be sure to also check links in your Web pages to make sure they send surfers where you mean for them to go.

Nonprofit Publications What You Need to Know to Create Winning Publications

TIPS FOR TAKING, MANAGING AND INCORPORATING PHOTOS

The power of photography and other visual images can evoke emotion. Photographs can awaken memories or send a message about now. They can surface both happiness and sadness, hatred or compassion. They can capture attention and even compel someone to read an article that might not otherwise be read. There's both an art and a science to your use of photography and other visual images in the publications you produce.

Photography Tips to Help Capture Memorable Images

A photo may or may not speak a thousand words, but images that truly capture the focus of your organization help you communicate with the public in a way that copy cannot. Here are five ways to effectively use photography to relay a compelling message:

1. **Look beyond the obvious for subjects.** While many supporters want to see pictures of your gala event, also include some shots leading up to the big day with candid snaps of volunteers doing tasks like setting up tables, making decorations or brainstorming. Show the thought and effort of those who made it possible.

2. **Be a roving photojournalist.** Walk around your facility with a camera to visit departments and quietly take a few pictures of people at work. Zoom in on the aide tenderly helping seat an elderly man at the cafeteria table, or reading a story to a happy preschooler. You can follow up to get releases if you get material that's too good not to use.

Great photos can help you communicate in a way that copy cannot.

3. **Choose some of the best images, then use them extensively.** When you have a collection of outstanding images, use them for print, Web and television advertising, and with news releases or brochures. Frequent exposure over time continues to positively connect with the community.

4. **Look for background objects that date or clutter the image.** Your new wing is ready for press photos. Avoiding parked cars, snowy sidewalks and holiday decorations will make the photos more versatile for all-purpose use. Choose a sunny, dry day and a time when traffic is minimal to take the picture. You may be able to use it for years.

5. **Take time to pose subjects.** Get more mileage out of great pictures by ensuring that all subjects look their best and like the shot. Arrange the group and tell them you will be smoothing hair and straightening collars as needed — most will be grateful. Take at least five or six pictures to increase the odds that at least one will be flattering of everyone.

Stock Up for Child-friendly Photo Shoot

Taking photos of babies or children? Brace yourself — it's not easy!

Key ingredients to a successful photo shoot with the younger set — along with lots of patience — are child-friendly props. Props that you can use behind the scenes and possibly in the photo as well help to engage children — bringing forth animated, smiling faces — and entertain them as they await their turn before the camera.

Here are some props to consider when planning a photo shoot with children (be prepared to send items home with children):

- Spill-proof containers of bubbles
- Sidewalk chalk
- Stickers
- Beach balls and colorful sunglasses

- Fuzzy mittens, hats and Styrofoam snowballs
- Sports balls and other sports props
- Child-safe musical instruments

- Mylar balloons (avoid latex due to choking and allergy risks)
- Stuffed animals
- Bowls of shiny apples or other colorful fruit

Boost Photo Quantity, Quality to Make Publications Pop

The proliferation of digital camera technology means that more people than ever may be taking photos for your organization's publications and website. But just because someone owns a camera doesn't make him/her a photographer.

Whether you're the one taking the photos, you're delegating the task to other staff members or volunteers, or you're inviting the public to share your photos from our special event, consider these tips for getting the best possible images, which come from Brent Goodrich, media relations manager, Make-A-Wish Foundation of America (Phoenix, AZ):

Here are some tried-and-tested tips for getting the best possible images

1. **Don't be shy with your subjects.** Get one to two steps closer than you normally would. This allows you to fill the frame.

2. **Shoot at your subject's eye level.** This will minimize foreshortening and distortion.

3. **When taking photos outdoors, shoot subjects in open shade, not in direct sunlight.** This minimizes squinting while keeping them cool and comfortable.
   If necessary, use fill-in flash to illuminate the subject.

4. **When using a digital camera, set the image resolution to its maximum level (3-5 MB per picture).**

5. **Take many, many pictures.** It is always better to take too many pictures than to take too few. This will insure you get the best possible shots. (Remember, when using a digital camera, you have no film cost associated with taking extra pictures, so shoot away!)

6. **Create a tip sheet for your organization's photographers,** such as the wallet card below, which Goodrich uses to help volunteers and constituents contribute quality materials for his organization's publications.

Source: Brent Goodrich, Media Relations Manager, Make-A-Wish Foundation of America, Phoenix, AZ. Phone (602) 279-9474. E-mail: bgoodrich@wish.org

Volunteers and supporters of Make-A-Wish Foundation of America (Phoenix, AZ) are better prepared to bring back quality photos, thanks to this two-sided wallet card of tips, co-created by communications department staff and Brent Goodrich, media relations manager.

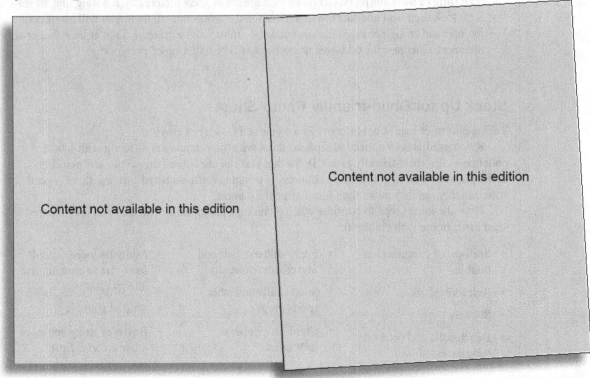

Content not available in this edition

Content not available in this edition

Tell Your Organization's Story Through Photos

Use images of your facilities, people and programs to tell the story of your cause.

Staff with the University of San Francisco (USF) of San Francisco, CA, did just that by creating a 61-photo day-in-the-life slideshow for USF's print and online magazines.

"This was a fun way for our readers to experience a slice of life on campus," says Angie Davis, director of communications, USF School of Law and former editor of USF Magazine. "Many of our 80,000 readers, who are primarily alumni, haven't visited campus recently. We wanted to convey the vibrancy of our campus community, the diversity of our people and programs, how our mission is lived out on a daily basis, and just what it's like to spend a day on campus."

Two freelance photographers and one in-house photographer shot the images, taking a combined 1,400 photos in one day.

"We negotiated a standard full-day rate that included print and Web use of the photos," says Davis.

Planning which areas of campus would be photographed and at what times took roughly one month to coordinate. Doing so involved steps such as working with professors whose classes they wanted to photograph in action and determining where landscapers would be planting trees that day.

"I came up with a rough schedule of events and activities including classes, sporting events, lectures and rehearsals that were scheduled on the photo day, and I split up the assignments among the photographers," says Davis. "I also built in plenty of time for them to explore and roam the campus to capture the unplanned, spontaneous moments.

"Once the photos came back, I worked with our in-house team of four graphic designers to choose which photos to include in the magazine."

They shared the finished product in print and electronic versions of the magazine and on USF's intranet. Some photos shot during the day have been used in admissions brochures.

"We received very positive feedback from the campus community and readers, who said (the day-in-the-life feature) gave them a vivid picture of life at USF," says Davis. "One staff member told me it reminded him of why he is so proud to be a part of this university."

For organizations thinking of creating a photo story, Davis offers this advice, "The key is finding the right balance between having enough scheduled activities and events, and allowing enough free time for the photographers to use their own instincts in capturing spontaneous moments. I would recommend using photographers whose strength is in photojournalism."

Source: Angie Davis, Director of Communications, University of San Francisco, School of Law, San Francisco, CA. Phone (415) 422-4409.

Photo Tour Showcases New Addition

Spotlight your new or enhanced facility with an online photo tour like the one used by Covenant Hospice (Pensacola, FL) to promote a building addition.

"Warm brownies, birthday parties, family gatherings and places for family to bond are all unexpected sites at the residence," says Don Ruth, director of communications. To encourage persons to make in-person visits and experience the site firsthand, Ruth says, they promoted an online photo tour showcasing the facility's warm, inviting atmosphere.

During the addition's construction, Melissa Chapman, multimedia specialist, conducted two 30-minute photo shoots to document the progress and collect images for the photo tour. She utilized the photo album features built into the hospice's content management system, called Tendenci, to create the tour.

"Because we are a nonprofit, it was not feasible to purchase video equipment or hardware to create professional panoramic tours," says Chapman. "With basic photography equipment and Web tools, we are able to update patients, families, donors and the community as to the progress of our new addition in ways that a written description can't convey."

They notified donors by direct mail about the addition and invited them to take the online and in-person tours.

Chapman cites one unexpected perk of the online feature. Persons attending open houses "were excited to be able to go back home and show additional family members what they got to see" by logging on to the online photo tour.

Sources: Don Ruth, Director of Communications; Melissa Chapman, Multimedia Specialist; Covenant Hospice, Pensacola, FL. Phone (850) 433-2155.

Create Photo Archive That Is Accessible, Searchable

Whether your organization has been around for one year or 100, chances are you have many photos showcasing achievements, milestones and, most importantly, your mission in action.

Chances are also that your photo filing system could use a little help.

Establishing an easy-to-use system for archiving photos will benefit your entire staff by streamlining the process of searching for and using your photos. Doing so may also inspire you to use the photos in a new, valuable way, such as creating an online scrapbook or historical timeline.

Consider Software Program Designed to Organize Digital Photos

Do you have a user-friendly system for archiving current and older photos?

While a number of computer software programs target digital photo organization, here's a system that is working well for communications staff at Antioch University New England (Keene, NH).

"We have about 7,000 digital photos on the server," says Sean Wiley, assistant director of communications. "Originally, these were organized in folders with names descriptive enough to lead you to the right place, if you already knew the system."

But increasing numbers of photos in the digital archive created the need to offer additional organizational tools, he says.

So they invested in Extensis Portfolio software.

"This software is life-changing," says Wiley. "We've gone from barely controlled chaos and having to open large files across the network, to a system of keywords and sub-galleries that will get better the more time we put into it."

Wiley cites two specific factors that created the need to be more proactive and systematic in cataloging the collection: The huge growth of digital photography; and greater involvement of other constituencies in choosing images. "The Web developers, the academic departments, development and others wanted to be able to browse the collection," he says.

The software has proven to be a worthwhile solution, allowing improved access and organization, Wiley says. "A photo can be tagged with as many keywords as might make sense down the road. A group of students sitting with books outside might be tagged Students, Study, Group, [name of academic program], Green, Outdoors, etc.," says Wiley. "All the photos are shown as thumbnails, and viewable in full screen mode. These are not the huge, cumbersome original files, but elements of an easy-to-use database which is not unlike navigating Flickr (www.flickr.com)."

Antioch communications staff began using the Portfolio software toward the end of 2007. They loaded the software onto a computer that is dedicated to photo management. The cost of the version of the software used by the university was $199. For more information about this software, including the server-based version, visit www.extensis.com.

Computer-based Photo Data System Improves Access for All Staff

The process of importing the photos into the software was a simple one. "You can drag folders onto the Portfolio window to import," says Wiley. "The originals live on the server; the thumbnails and tags and database information live on the local machine. You need only deal with the original files when placing images in the Quark file or sending it to the Web folk."

Wiley says organizing the photos is saving time and energy throughout the university staff.

"When someone from an academic department can browse the collection at their speed, choose candidates and create their own little gallery, it both saves us time and really lets them be a bigger part of the process," he says. "There might be a fixed idea about which are the good photos from a shoot two years ago, but now that we can speedily look through everything, we might find some gems that fit new needs."

Source: Sean Wiley, Assistant Director of Communications, Antioch University New England, Keene, NH. Phone (603) 283-2431. Website: www.antiochne.edu

Get Creative With Staff Photos

Websites for many organizations include professional head shots of staff members. If such an approach is a little too tame for your organization, consider more creative ways to capture the essence of your staff.

Online visitors seeking information on the public affairs and communications (PubCom) staff at Lewis & Clark College, (Portland, OR) don't see their faces.

They see their feet.

On the Who We Are staff page (www.lclark.edu/dept/pubcom/), photos next to staff members' names, titles and contact information show their feet. Most persons are wearing shoes, while one has shoeless feet in brightly colored socks.

Amy Drill, art director, says she has taken photos of her own feet, to document her travels, for more than 20 years. So when the associate vice president of public affairs and communications came on board, she created a welcome book PDF to familiarize him with the PubCom staff. The book included pictures of staff members' feet along with brief bios.

When the time came to update the department's webpage, Drill thought to include the foot photos again.

She says the photos reflect the creative nature of the department staff — persons who are professional while also having fun and maintaining a sense of curiosity. While everyone on the staff was on board with the foot photos, she cautions against including photos your staff may not feel comfortable having published. "If they are not willing to go along with the idea then it obviously does not reflect them as a group."

As a rule of thumb, she says, avoid using photos that could offend internal or external audiences or that show staff engaging in unprofessional behavior.

Other ideas of photos to include along with staff listings are: an image of each staff member's favorite spot on your campus; a picture of his or her pet; key chain; a childhood photo or shot of a favorite keepsake kept on his or her desk.

Board Member Photos

Need to update photos of individual board members? Try this, rather than doing the usual (and boring) head-and-shoulder shots, take individual photos of board members doing whatever they consider to be favorite pastimes: fishing, cooking, volunteering, playing with a grandchild, etc. The board members will have fun sharing a favorite interest, and you'll have the makings of a great human interest story.

In choosing a photo theme, "Organizations have to be honest about why they are doing it and what would reflect them well," Drill says. "Don't try to get cute with what you are doing if it doesn't reflect your reality; if you are creative, be creative, and if you are serious, then be serious."

Source: Amy Drill, Art Director, Public Affairs and Communications, Lewis & Clark College, Portland, OR. Phone (503) 768-7973.

Use Professional Headshots in a Variety of Ways

Once you've gone to the trouble to have professional headshots taken of your staff, board members and others key to your organization's success, look for places to use the photos beyond your website.

For example, when corresponding with donors or other contacts, have the sender insert his/her photo onto the electronic version of your organization's letterhead. This can be especially beneficial when reaching out to new contacts.

In addition, having a library of professional staff headshots will come in handy when dealing with media contacts. If a reporter is doing a story on your organization or a specific staff member, offer to e-mail a professional headshot to include with the story. Of course, keep in mind that you may need to obtain the photographer's permission, and/or give the photographer written credit, to use headshots in ways other than originally discussed.

Fees for professional headshots vary but generally cost several hundred dollars. Photographers may charge sitting or travel fees, so ask about all costs in advance.

Make Most of Mug Shots

If you take employee mug shots, how do you handle it when someone shows up looking less than professional or just doesn't photograph well?

Remember your job is to portray your organization — and its representatives — in the best light. Then use your communication talents to make suggestions to improve the person's profile. For example, if someone shows up in a T-shirt, say: "It's my experience that a shirt with a collar (and tie) makes for a better photo. Can you come back later today/same time tomorrow with one?"

For someone with a bad hair day, do your best to make it look presentable. If that doesn't help, say, "I'd like a polished look for this photo, but I'm worried the camera may make your hairstyle look too casual. Can you set up a trim/style and come back?"

For the woman with no makeup (or makeup that's over the top), blame it on the camera or lighting as well. "This flash just washes people out (or overemphasizes makeup), and I'm worried you will look pale (your makeup will look overdone). Can you please put on lipstick and blush to help make your photo pop a bit more (or can we tone down your blush and eyeshadow just a bit)?"

Another trick? Stock up on props to help people look their best. Hang a mirror up in your office and add a shelf with a comb, trial-size hair spray and neutral-tone lipstick samples. Keep a well-pressed dress shirt, blazer, one-size-fits-all turtleneck or shirt-collar (dickey) to give your subject the professional look you want to portray.

Finally, when taking a mugshot, don't let the subject stand flat against the wall. Ask him/her to step out at least three feet from the neutral-patterned background, turn his/her shoulders at a slight angle while pointing his/her face toward the camera.

Simple Tips Lead to Stunning Photos

Public relations professionals wear many hats, including that of photographer. If the newspaper needs a headshot of your executive director or if your agency hosts an event, chances are you or one of your staff persons will end up shooting the picture.

Andrew McAllister, professional photographer with Andrew McAllister Photography LLC (Akron, OH), shares tips to get the most out of your pictures, whether you're professionally trained or picking up a point-and-shoot digital camera for the first time:

- **Determine photo context before hitting the shutter.** What is the tone of the story or placement of the photo? Should your CEO be smiling or take a more serious tone?

- **Background matters!** Don't line your subject up against a wall. McAllister suggests using a larger room with lots of natural light.

- **Know your camera.** Read the manual and find out what the camera can do. Practice in different situations so when necessary, you can get the best shot in the shortest time.

- **Get in the action and get people's faces.** We've all seen the pictures of people's backs in agency newsletters. McAllister says to get in the middle of the moment to snap photos that capture the event's feeling and tone. Shoot early in the event when attendees are more energetic.

- **When all else fails...find someone who wants to be a pro.** Check out local photography programs for persons who may be willing to volunteer to shoot portfolio shots of your board and staff and also take casual shots of your special event.

Encourage Others to Interpret Your Photos

Here are three ideas to obtain quality images to celebrate and promote your cause:

1. **Sponsor a photography contest.** Chances are you have amateur photographers among your volunteers, donors, employees and community. Challenge them to capture meaningful images of your organization's facets or people. Offer prizes, even if the reward is only special recognition. Submit top photos to your local newspaper with a press release about the winners and information about your organization.

2. **Ask a variety of professionals to donate one photograph each.** Send professional photographers or artists a request for their interpretations of your organization's role in the community. Use images in a poster, calendar, booklet, annual report or campaigns for months or years to come. Treat each participant as an in-kind donor, naming him/her in newsletters and individually with each use of the donated work.

3. **Think big.** If you are about to observe an anniversary, gather as many supporters, employees and volunteers as you can to pose and create the numeral (e.g., 25) in human form for an overhead group photo. Make posters, postcards and prints that can be purchased as souvenirs and used in advertising. Such photos are entertaining as people look for themselves in the crowd and create an esprit d'corps as well.

Source: Andrew McAllister, Photographer, Andrew McAllister Photography LLC, Akron, OH.
Phone (330) 687-6364. E-mail: info@andrewfoto.com. Website: www.andrewfoto.com

Nonprofit Publications: What You Need to Know to Create Winning Publications.
Edited by Scott C. Stevenson.
© 2010 Stevenson, Inc. Published 2010 by Stevenson, Inc.

Nonprofit Publications What You Need to Know to Create Winning Publications

LAYOUT AND DESIGN IDEAS

One should approach publication layout and design in the same way that you do writing: Identify your audience, define your purpose and communicate your message. When you're writing, you present information in a logical order, so do the same when you lay out each page or panel of each publication or brochure. Recognize that your publication should grab the person's attention first, then keep them reading.

Reinforce Your Brand With Striking Images

Display striking photos that show your organization's mission in action to further your branding efforts and inspire staff, visitors, donors and volunteers.

In December 2008, staff with Lutheran World Relief (LWR) of Baltimore, MD hung three high-impact photos in their lobby. The 20 X 30-inch, color framed images (shown at left) show participants in LWR development projects around the world.

"The primary reason we put up the photos was to reinforce our brand identity as a global organization," says Emily Sollie, director, communication & media relations. "We also hoped they'd be inspirational in a broad sense, capturing happy, self-empowered people from different cultures and contexts, and in various stages of life, who all have a brighter outlook on the future. The hope is that the photos help remind people, both staff and visitors, of our organizational mission and vision, and ultimately why we do the work that we do."

Communications staff selected about 40 photos from their image database as candidates for the display. Eight staff members reviewed the photos and made recommendations as to which should be displayed.

"The leadership team endorsed those recommendations and the photos were approved for display by the building committee," says Daniel Lee, director, marketing. The images were enlarged by a print shop and matted and framed by a local framing business.

"The anecdotal feedback received thus far has been overwhelmingly positive," he notes. "Our staff and guests appreciate the change in decor, but especially like how captivating and inviting the new images are."

When selecting images to display in your lobby or other area, the LWR officials say, look for high quality images capable of being enlarged without loss of quality. Be sure you have permission of the subjects to use their images in a promotional manner.

Finally, consider asking staff members, participants, volunteers and others to weigh in on which images they feel represent your brand in a positive and inspiring way.

Content not available in this edition

Content not available in this edition

Content not available in this edition

Images of persons whose lives are made better thanks to the work of Lutheran World Relief take center stage at the organization's Baltimore, MD headquarters.

Source: Daniel Lee, Director, Marketing; Emily Sollie, Director, Communication & Media Relations; Lutheran World Relief, Baltimore, MD. Phone (410) 230-2800. E-mail: DLee@lwr.org or ESollie@lwr.org

Visual Theme Intrigues Readers, Connects Them With Organization's History

Creating a visual theme for publications by repeatedly using a familiar image will strike a chord with your readers and serve as a valuable design element.

Oranges and citrus trees are unifying tools for the annual report for Saint Leo University (Saint Leo, FL), says Susan Shoulet, director of public relations. The images also play up the university's history. Founded in 1889 by Benedictine monks, the main campus is surrounded by citrus groves. "I've often heard stories about how the monks sold the oranges to help support the school in lean economic times," Shoulet says. "We knew alumni would connect with the trees and the oranges."

The university's signature colors of green and gold further the citrus grove tradition, says Shoulet, noting that this is the second year the university has used the design theme in the annual report.

"It's more subtle than just oranges or orange trees on each page," she says. "The first thing we did was to create a template with some style rules for the entire publication; color, fonts, and some basic design elements that were to be used throughout the publication.

"When we designed the first report, I knew the use of the orange slices and segments on the financial report page might be a little risky, but since we published the first report, I've only heard good things about the design."

The report goes to all university alumni, numbering more than 50,000, so design appeal was crucial, Shoulet notes. "It has to appeal to alumni who have never set foot on the campus here in Florida, and it has to represent the university as a unified organization, she says.

"We think we achieved that through the annual report's design and content."

Shoulet, who has a graphic design background, came up with the concept of utilizing the orange tree images in the report. The 2006-2007 annual report was designed by an outside freelance designer, and the 2007-2008 report, by the in-house graphic designer, both incorporate stock and original images.

When choosing a visual theme for your publication, choose images that are meaningful to your organization and will resonate with your supporters, Shoulet advises. "Look to the past for concepts and images; look to the future for how you will apply them to the publication."

Source: Susan Shoulet, Director of Public Relations, Saint Leo University, Saint Leo, FL.
Phone (352) 588-8121.
E-mail: susan.shoulet@saintleo.edu

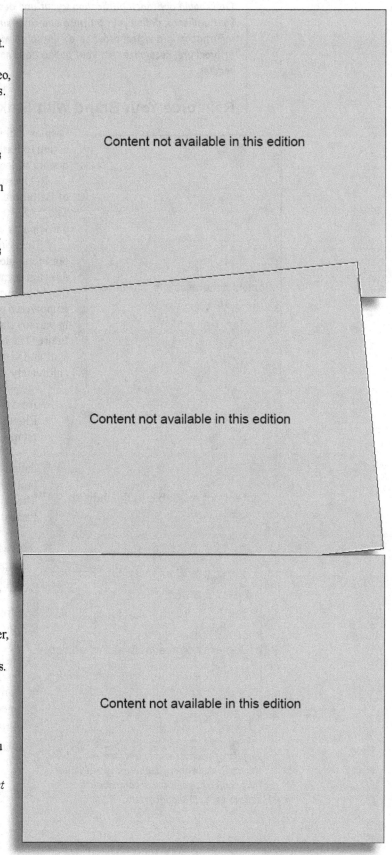

Content not available in this edition

Content not available in this edition

Content not available in this edition

How to Design a Winning Brochure

Creating a knockout brochure that provides your community with an innovative design will pique their interest in your new endeavor.

When Aimee Keegan, public relations manager, AHRC Nassau (Brookville, NY), began working on their Galaxy of Hope brochure last year, she began by lining out the goals of the piece with staff members. "I meet with the director of community resources to discuss what kind of brochure we're planning on doing, what our goals are, what kind of budget we can work with and anything else she would like to highlight. I work with other staff members to decide what we're looking to achieve, the population we're addressing, what colors or themes we would like to use, etc. It's a real team effort."

By having clear goals regarding how each brochure should be designed and distributed, your organization will create a focused piece suitable for the target community. "The goal is always to make an attractive piece that will stand out from other mailings people may receive. Of course the most important component is the piece's functionality — whether it's a direct mail piece or an informational brochure," says Keegan.

Whether your organization uses a template or designs each brochure with a unique layout, deciding how the design will work in various formats is essential. "I start from scratch every time. Sometimes I borrow things from printed materials that I think would work best with our brochure. I make it suitable for printing and mailing and we usually put a PDF on the website," says Keegan.

Creating a winning brochure that clearly orchestrates your organization's goals, whether you're working towards collecting donations, obtaining event participants or feedback, can be a demanding project. "The brochure has to be attractive and draw in the reader. The information must be presented in a concise manner but in a compassionate way that makes the person receiving it want to get involved with AHRC," says Keegan.

Source: Aimee C. Keegan, Public Relations Manager, AHRC Nassau, Brookville, NY.
Phone (516) 626-1000 ext. 1134. E-mail: akeegan@ahrc.org

It's important to have clear goals about how each brochure should be designed and distributed.

Make Your Newsletter Visually Appealing

Does your nonprofit's newsletter lack visual appeal?

Senior Editor Joyce Remy, CARESOURCE Healthcare Communications (Seattle, WA), says there are five ways nonprofits can improve its newsletter appearance:

1. **Start with a great overall newsletter design or redesign.** "If you've been doing the same thing for years and years, it might be time to consider using a professional at this stage," says Remy. If money is tight, redesign the newsletter in-house or ask donors who might have designers on staff to contribute their talents.

2. **Target a look and feel that best represents your organization.** "Glitzy is not necessarily best, if, for example, you are a grassroots organization," she says. "A high-end art magazine look might not inspire confidence that donations go to the services you provide."

3. **Shoot for a unified look and feel.** "Just because you can use a bunch of fonts and colors doesn't mean you should," Remy says. Remember a few basic rules when designing a newsletter: 1) Keep your basic design consistent from issue to issue, with some elements always appearing in the same place; 2) Stick with two or three strong typefaces that go well together; 3) Break up long articles with sidebars, pull quotes and graphics; and 4) If using stock images, avoid the temptation to use too many unrelated styles.

4. **Photos draw the eye.** "A bad photo is worse than no photo," says Remy. "In this age of digital photography, you can find out on the spot whether you've got a good shot." Provide tip sheets for your amateur photographers and set cameras to the highest resolution possible."

5. **If you post a PDF of your newsletter online, preview the document to ensure fonts and images have been converted correctly.**

Here are five ways to add visual appeal to your organization's newsletter.

Source: Joyce Remy, Senior Editor, CARESOURCE Healthcare Communications, Seattle, WA.
Phone (800) 448-5213. E-mail: remy@caresource.com

Match Paper Weight and Finish to Your Publication

In the world of publications, few moments can be more disappointing than getting a job back and realizing it is on the wrong type of paper — paper that's too limp, heavy, textured or slick — because you failed to thoroughly research paper choices.

Here are steps to help you better match paper to the project at hand:

1. **Address your paper choice at the start.** Talk to your printer about size before you go to design and layout. Your printer may tell you that a minimal change will allow the layout to fit better on the sheet and reduce your printing bill. Adjusting your layout early will also save layout time.

2. **Decide what impression you want to make.** As a nonprofit that depends on charitable support, you may want to avoid a premium paper that looks like you went all out. If not using photos, consider recycled paper with visible fibers. For true color and crisp images, a coated matte finish is a good choice. For a softer understated image, uncoated papers provide a nice base for four-color printing.

3. **Should your cover be white or a color?** Colored stock can make for an impressive cover, especially if combined with blind embossing, foil stamping or a die-cut window revealing an image on the inside. If choosing white for both cover and inside, know that ink will stand out on a brighter whiter stock, while a warmer tone of white can be easier to read (an important consideration for the over-40 crowd).

4. **Opt for heavier weights for brochures and booklets.** Light cover stocks are common choices for brochures today. For brochures in display racks, you'll appreciate a heavier stock that holds its shape rather than flopping over. A word of caution; heavier stock needs to be scored before folding and can produce unsightly cracks at folds. Discuss this with your printer before you decide on weight.

5. **Choose heavier paper for tabloids.** If printing a tabloid, consider using a white 60# stock rather than newsprint or 50#. The extra weight will help your ink coverage look better and avoid a bleed-through look.

6. **Get advice from your printer and graphic designer.** Ask your printer for sample sheets of paper the size of your project. Ask your graphic designer, if you have one, to educate you, too.

7. **When in doubt, collect samples from others.** Include ideas that you believe work well along with those that you think represent a situation in which another type of paper would have worked better.

Planning Your Brochure

Before you begin writing and designing a brochure, answer these critical questions:

- ✓ What is the brochure's objective?
- ✓ Who is your audience? Students? Patients? Would-be donors?
- ✓ What key information and messages do you want included?

Document Design Changes

When redesigning print or online resources, make sure to document the changes you make. Doing so will help give you perspective, chart your progress and inspire you to continually improve the appearance of your materials.

If you are redesigning your website, take screenshots of the old layout so you can keep track of design and content changes throughout the years.

The same goes for changing your logo or brochure art work. Keep digital or paper copies when appropriate to use as reference materials for future projects. These copies will serve as valuable records for years to come.

If you haven't documented your website over the years but would like to see how far you've come, log on to www.archive.org — a free online Internet library — and use the Wayback Machine feature to view snapshots of your website over the years.

Dollar Bill Rule of Design

What's black, white and unread? The newsletter that's heavy on plain text blocks and light on design elements.

Use this trick to check your design.

Place a dollar bill on your full-sized layout. Does it cover several elements? Or does it just touch large areas of plain, 12-point text? If just text, look at adding subheads, a boxed quote, photo, bullet points, logo or other graphic element to break up space and boost reader interest.

Use Well-known Faces to Garner Publicity

Do you have graduates, donors, staff, active volunteers or supporters who are well known?

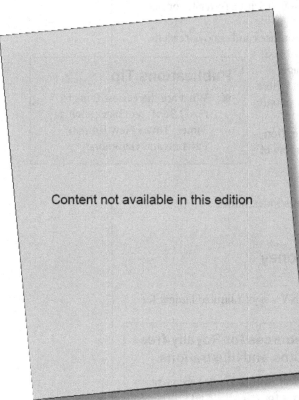

Content not available in this edition

Spotlight them in your promotional materials to generate publicity for your organization.

"We feature successful graduates of Trinity in our admissions recruiting materials, including Cathie Black, president of Hearst Magazines, which publishes Oprah magazine, Good Housekeeping and many other familiar names among magazines," says Ann Pauley, vice president for institutional advancement, Trinity Washington University (Washington, DC). "We want to show prospective students the kinds of successful role models that Trinity Washington University educates."

Showcasing successful alumni and others connected to your organization can have long-lasting positive effects.

"In fall 2007, we enrolled the largest freshman class in 40 years," and in fall 2008, had an all-time enrollment high, Pauley says. "Obviously, there are many factors involved, including hard work on the part of our admissions staff, strategic communications, careful follow-up, successful open houses, etc. But marketing materials are definitely a factor, and featuring successful graduates in those materials is part of that strategy."

The university has been featuring outstanding alumni in marketing materials for many years in a variety of ways, including:

- Admissions materials, including brochures and newsletters, be photos, interviews and descriptions of these stellar graduates' achievements.

- On the university's homepage, a rotating Profiles of Success feature, which includes stories and photos of successful, well-known graduates.

When spotlighting a well-known member of the community in publicity efforts, be sure to obtain permission to use the person's likeness, quotes and other personal information. You may wish to meet with them in person for interviews or photo sessions.

Pauley says that the university occasionally arranges for photo sessions with featured graduates to obtain images for certain materials, in addition to using photos of the graduates already used in feature articles in the university magazine.

She advises choosing people who are at different levels of their career and who will appeal to a wide audience. Along with using the highly visible Cathie Black, they have also featured Perita Carpenter, a producer for ABC News who is a more recent graduate.

"High school students will relate better to more recent graduates, but they are also impressed by those graduates who are at the top of their careers," says Pauley.

Tying successful individuals to your organization will show the community how hardworking and unique you are.

"We receive positive feedback from prospective students, parents and guidance counselors when they see who some of our successful graduates are," says Pauley. "That gives them confidence that Trinity provides a high quality educational experience with an emphasis on women's leadership skills."

Source: Ann Pauley, Vice President for Institutional Advancement, Trinity Washington University, Washington, DC. Phone (202) 884-9725.

Reserve Special Fonts for Special Occasions

Fun, creative fonts have their place. For example, if you're hosting a renaissance fair, a great way to attract attention and send a consistent message is to use a font with a romantic or old-world flair in flyers, posters and internal publications.

But too many fonts — or overuse of unusual fonts — just confuses and annoys readers. Establish a single, clean font style for most of your headlines and text. Vary from this style only when doing so strengthens your message.

Think of specialty type fonts as spices — a sprinkle here and there can make a good publication great, but overdoing it could leave people turning up their noses.

That being said, if you're looking for a special font or inspiration, do a Web search using the terms free font download. Here are a few of sites you'll find:

- www.acidfonts.com
- www.all-free-fonts.com
- www.fontvillage.com
- www.rotodesign.com/fonts/index.html
- www.dafont.com
- www.freefontsnow.com

Publications Tip

- What are the easiest fonts to read? Serif typefaces such as Times, Times New Roman, Palatino and Garamond.

Tips for Making Your Design Sing for Less Money

Looking to cut costs without sacrificing quality?

Laura Rogers, art director, Dandelion Design (Rensselaer, NY), says a limited budget for collateral materials doesn't have to mean dull design.

Here, Rogers shares five tips she uses to help her nonprofit clients save big bucks, while still making a lasting impression:

1. **Use royalty-free photography and illustrations.** Rogers says many online resources are available for this (see box, at right).

2. **Never create or ask for a three-color design,** which could significantly boost production costs. A three-color job, she says, "can't be printed on a two-color press, or if you do use a two-color press (for such a job), they have to run the job through twice."

Resources for Royalty-free Photos and Illustrations

The following websites are great options for affordable art:
www.gettyimages.com
www.istockphoto.com
www.shutterstock.com
www.illustrationworks.com
www.stockillustrationsource.com
www.clipart.com

3. **Consider using four-color, but only for the cover,** where it will catch people's attention and you'll get the biggest bang for your production buck. The rest of the publication can still be done in black and white.

4. **When using only one or two ink colors, incorporate a special paper stock to add some splash.** If possible, make one ink color a metallic. "There's a small up charge," she says, "but along with a neat sheet of paper, your design could sing for little money."

5. **When possible, design materials such as business cards and letterhead as a shell or template for future jobs related to your brand.** "You can spend the money once and get a nice template printed at a higher quantity for a better cost," Rogers says. "Then, as you need them customized, just imprint in black."

Throughout all print production, Rogers says, the basics for cost-effective design still apply, including designing for standard-size papers, using off-the-shelf envelopes and avoiding bleeds. Applying one or two of the additional tips cited above, the art director says, will help you to take your publications to the next level while staying within budget.

Save big bucks by implementing these cost-saving ideas.

Source: Laura Rogers, Art Director, Dandelion Design, Rensselaer, NY. Phone (518) 283-9474. E-mail: lea@dandedesign.com

How can you decide between a hardcopy publication and one that's online? Should you offer both? Should you target online publications to particular segments of your database? How can online pubs help ease your budget crunch? These and other questions are addressed in this chapter.

E-publication Pros, Cons

Most nonprofit organizations produce a wide variety of publications, many of which are e-publications that exist only in electronic format.

Sharing their thoughts on the pros and cons of producing e-publications are Warren Bell, associate vice president, university and media relations, and Richard Tucker, director of publications (print and online), at Xavier University of Louisiana (New Orleans, LA).

Positives of E-publications:

Before launching a new e-publication, weigh its pros and cons.

- Publishing online makes printing current items easier as you are not faced with time and labor associated with producing hard copy materials, plus there is no lag time for printing and distribution.
- If you make a mistake, it is easily correctable online, whereas in print, the mistake is in stone forever.
- Inexpensive to produce or distribute.
- Speed of delivery — in most cases, gets to where you want in seconds.
- Somewhat easier to lay out than print publications, depending on the form and format used.

Negatives of E-publications:

- Not everyone can receive e-publications. Believe it or not, not everyone has an e-mail address.
- Even many persons with e-mail addresses don't want additional stuff sent to their e-mail accounts.
- Many people prefer hard copies they can hold in their hands. Case in point – Xavier has a postal mailing list of more than 15,000 alums, and yet, the e-mail list is under 4,000.
- Limited shelf life — Once e-mail newsletter is read, it is most likely deleted by reader, whereas a printed piece might survive for a few months on the family coffee table and/or corporate or foundation lobby.

Sources: Richard L. Tucker, Director of Publications (print & online); Warren A. Bell, Jr., Associate Vice President, University & Media Relations; Xavier University of Louisiana, New Orleans, LA. Phone (504) 486-7411. Website: www.xula.edu/institutional-advancement/index.php

Seek E-mail Addresses from Newsletter Recipients

Are you considering offering an electronic newsletter to donors, constituents or other key audiences soon? Now's the time to start gathering e-mail addresses.

It's wise to exhaust every technique for gathering your constituents' e-mail address.

Even if you plan to keep sending traditional paper newsletters through regular mail, gathering e-mail addresses for those on your mailing list is a good idea. You could use e-mails to test online solicitations, newsletters or as a means to invite supporters to special events.

Here are three ways to start gathering e-mail addresses:

1. Include a call to action in your current newsletter to send an e-mail to be entered in a contest, seek important information — or better yet, receive a free gift.

2. When registering people for special events or fundraisers, ask for their e-mail addresses as well.

3. On your website, prominently feature a button that says Yes, I want to get the latest information by e-mail that links to a simple sign-up form.

Cater e-newsletter Content to Target Audiences

. How do you target various audiences to get your message out?

"One way is through e-newsletters. Calvin College (Grand Rapids, MI) has four — Calvin Wire, which offers breaking news and alumni updates; Calvin-Parents (for parents of students); Calvin-Sports Report (featuring the latest on college athletes) and Calvin-Connection, which has information about on-campus programs and events open to the public. This allows us to send our message directly to our constituents, while reaching very distinct audiences. We determined it would be more widely read if the publications were specific to the audience.

"We are also able to inform and remind neighbors and friends about learning opportunities at or sponsored by Calvin and increase attendance at these events, while allowing us to promote photo galleries and video too.

"Feedback has been mostly positive. We get a lot of thank-yous and many people stay on the lists long after their child has graduated.

"Our distribution frequency varies from twice a month with Calvin Wire to daily for Calvin-Sports Report, with each publication going out to anywhere from 500 (Calvin-Connection) to 6,527 recipients (Calvin-Parents)."

Source: Lynn Rosendale, Associate Director Communications and Marketing, Calvin College, Grand Rapids, MI. Phone (616) 526-6861. E-mail: lrosenda@calvin.edu

Segment and target particular groups with e-communications that speak to them and their interests

How to Handle a Publicized Mistake

. **"Have you ever experienced a major newsletter blooper?"**

"Our e-newsletter for faculty and staff once featured a story on a professor who had received a teaching award. It wasn't long after sending out an e-mail to employees with a link to that issue that I received a voicemail message from a staff member. He said he was quite certain we had inserted the wrong photo to accompany the story on the professor. I pulled up the issue and gasped when I found myself staring at a headshot of Earvin 'Magic' Johnson, the former LA Lakers basketball star who had recently visited campus, instead of our distinguished professor, whose last name is Johnson. This was several years ago when our newsletter had just made the transition to an electronic format.

> "That's one benefit of electronic newsletters — corrections can be made immediately."

"I have a nice software program now, but back then I had to write stories with HTML code to signal paragraph breaks, italics, inserted images, etc. I can't recall now the technical explanation for what happened. There might have been two images in different folders — both named Johnson.jpg — and the wrong one showed up when the story was dropped into the template. Or, more likely, I inadvertently typed the wrong image tag. It was a quick fix to redirect to the proper photo. That's one benefit of electronic newsletters — corrections can be made immediately. I considered myself lucky that I only got the one call (and it wasn't from Professor Johnson).

"I printed out that newsletter and had it hanging on my office bulletin board for a long time as a reminder of a lesson learned. It's very funny in hindsight and I've shared lots of laughs with my colleagues over it. I'll never be accused of taking myself too seriously."

Has this ever happened to you?

— *Kristi Evans, News Director, Northern Michigan University, Marquette, MI*

Include a Toot-your-horn Section for Employees

Whether you distribute a print newsletter or an e-newsletter to employees, include a section that encourages employees to share accomplishments. Not only is it a good morale booster, but those accomplishments may provide information and story ideas that should be shared publicly.

Encourage employees to submit professional accomplishments prior to your scheduled deadline. Offer examples of what may be considered: appointments to boards; favorable program outcomes; published works and more.

Web-based Options Help Stop Communications Budget Drain

Whether to save on production costs, speed up dissemination of information or link to your supporters in the trendiest way possible, look for electronic, Web-based options to communicate with your constituency.

Turning to electronic options helped Shelly Grimes rise to a challenge her first day on the job as marketing and public relations coordinator for the Crossroads of America Council of the Boy Scouts of America (Indianapolis, IN), when she learned the organization's leaders felt they were receiving outdated information in their printed newsletters.

That was June 2007. Six months later, the council switched to electronic communications formatting, with the transition project staffed entirely by student volunteers from Indiana University-Purdue University Indianapolis (IUPUI).

The council now produces four versions of its monthly electronic newsletter for various audiences, including volunteers, parents and scouts. Grimes says print is an important component of the overall mix, and the group continues to produce a quarterly print newsletter for recognition and feature stories.

Budget was a secondary — though significant — consideration for transitioning to Web-based communications, Grimes says. "Not only was it a more cost-effective option, but it has served our leaders better. We've gotten overwhelmingly positive feedback," with newsletter subscriptions jumping from 4,000 to 7,600 in the 18 months since launch of the electronic vehicles.

The latest technological tools and toys can boost nonprofits' bottom lines beyond improving communications.

At St. Mary's Food Bank (Phoenix, AZ), for example, a global positioning system (GPS) purchased with grant money is helping organizers plan truck routes more efficiently and cut operating expenses. Program leaders project the collection of more goods without the need for additional trucks and employees, plus savings of $50,000 annually in fuel expenditures.

Postcard Replaces Newsletter in Blog-driven Option

Kivi Leroux Miller (Lexington, NC) president of EcoScribe Communications and Nonprofit Marketing Guide. com, advocates a balanced strategy of online communications and creative print tactics.

For example, in response to some nonprofit leaders lamenting they can only afford to send their print newsletters twice a year, Miller suggests creating full-color postcards, which — at one-third the cost of a four-page color newsletter — can go out six times a year for the same expenditure.

So effective is an attractive postcard, says Miller, that organizations may consider dropping newsletters altogether and augmenting the postcards with informative Web content.

Sources: Kivi Leroux Miller, author, Kivi's Nonprofit Communications Blog, Lexington, NC. Phone (336) 499-5816. E-mail: Kivi@ecoscribe.com. Blog: www.nonprofitmarketingguide.com/ blog/category/print-newsletters

Sources: Shelly Grimes, Marketing and Public Relations Coordinator, Crossroads of America Council/Boy Scouts of America, Indianapolis, IN. Phone 317-925-1900, ext. 224. E-mail: sgrimes@bsamail.org

Cut Down on Waste When Communicating With Others

Here are four ideas to conserve resources without compromising your message:

- **Offer a comprehensive online press kit.** While some media contacts may prefer a hard copy, make all materials available for download on your website and encourage contacts to refer to that version before requesting a printed copy.

- **Create online versions of your printed publications.** Depending on the number of readers you have, it may be worthwhile to ask your readers to opt for either the online or printed version of your publications. Some readers may still prefer receiving the hard copy in the mail; however, by offering a choice, you can cut the number of copies you print, which will also cut costs.

- **Recycle and encourage others to do so.** Remind your staff to recycle outdated business cards, correspondence or press materials. Include a line at the bottom of all printed materials asking the recipient to recycle any materials that they do not need to keep for future reference.

- **Think before you print.** Think twice before printing e-mails. Could the information be jotted down on scratch paper, stored in an online database or online calendar?

Cut Costs by Moving Annual Report Online

As printing costs continue to rise, more nonprofits are seeking alternative ways to reduce marketing expenditures. From newsletters to magazines to save-the-date cards, more and more communication pieces are moving from people's mailboxes to their e-mail inboxes.

Annual reports are no exception.

Mimi Koral, director of alumni communication, University of Pittsburgh (Pittsburgh, PA), says her office decided to abandon printing annual reports after determining that the nearly $65,000 being spent on printing and mailing an annual report was not justified.

"We weren't able to get a good gauge on whether we were getting the attention we were paying for," says Koral. "That's when we decided to go online only."

For two years, these online reports, which Koral describes as elaborate, featured messages from the chancellor and executive director; videos of students talking about the impact of scholarships in their lives; illustrated old and new Pitt traditions; and offered information on faculty projects and volunteer efforts.

"Going online with our annual report gave us the chance to shine light on all these aspects at the same time," says Koral.

They replaced the online annual report with an online streaming video of the chancellor's talk.

"After producing the first two online annual reports, we learned constructing the annual reports really ate up our webmaster's time," Koral says. "We realized our chancellor was touching on almost all the major points made in the annual report during his videotaped messages to alumni, so we decided to go with his talk only."

Koral's staff tapes the chancellor's five-minute talk in-house at a total production cost of about $7,500.

Koral publishes its Web page address in the university's paper publications and provides a link via the association's website. Alumni e-mail addresses are gathered from an online alumni directory and a company that searches public databases and matches e-mail addresses to alumni for whom the university does not have an e-mail address.

Save Money On Your Annual Report

Are you interested in cutting your printing costs by making your annual report available online only, but are worried that no one will follow it there? Any one of the following steps will make sure it still gets seen, while trimming your budget:

- ❑ **Good:** Send out a simple letter from your board president or CEO with a few highlights and a link to the report online.
- ❑ **Better:** Doing the same thing with a postcard will save you even more!
- ❑ **Best:** Sending an e-mail to your constituents, with the same info, would be the most cost-effective by far.

Another idea? Distribute a news release, highlighting one of your year's best stories or accomplishments, in conjunction with any of the above efforts.

Still can't imagine marketing without a hard copy? Do a short run with digital offset printing, which can be a way to get the quantity you need at an affordable price.

Source: Mimi Koral, Director of Alumni Communication, University of Pittsburgh, Pittsburgh, PA. Phone (412) 383-7078. E-mail: mimi.koral@ia.pitt.edu

E-zine Pros and Cons

Pam Wiley, communications officer, Mays Business School, Texas A&M University (College Station, TX), identifies the following benefits and pitfalls of implementing an e-zine.

"An e-zine is cost-effective when you have a lot of information, news or stories that can be produced to reach your target audience," says Wiley. Benefits of an e-zine include: the information is online; constituents and the public are able to gain access from anywhere; there are no printing or mailing costs; you have the ability to promote the organization worldwide; and mistakes in stories can be corrected immediately.

While e-zines are cost-effective and offer many advantages to an organization, Wiley says there are also pitfalls. They include: a constant need to develop information; must be refreshed at regular intervals; and you must promote the e-zine. "Just because something is on the Web doesn't mean your target audience knows about it," she says.

Source: Pam Wiley, Communications Officer, Mays Business School, Texas A&M University, College Station, TX. Phone (979) 845-0193. E-mail: psw@tamu.edu

Share Save-the-date Reminders in Your Publications, Online

Save-the-date cards can be an eye-catching way to promote your upcoming events.

In addition to mailing traditional cards, include save-the-date announcements in print and online publications as a low-cost way to reach a wider audience.

Staff at Providence Hospital (Washington, DC) routinely include such announcements for events put on by The Providence Health Foundation in the hospital's internal newsletter, which has a distribution of 2,880, and external newsletter, which has a distribution of 75,000, says Stephanie Hertzog, director, public relations.

These announcements, coupled with 700 mailed reminders, allow the hospital to reach an extremely large audience at a relatively low cost, Hertzog says. She notes that some of the 700 people included on the direct mail list also receive one of the newsletters, which serve as a second reminder of the upcoming event.

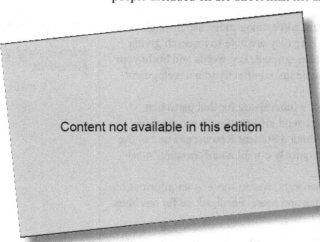

Content not available in this edition

Announcements are designed by a graphic artist who provides the hospital's publications manager with images to be used in both newsletters. Save-the-date announcements included in publications are usually identical to the mailed cards unless they need to be reformatted for print, and are placed in a section highlighting the foundation or on the back cover of the publication, depending on space.

When using save-the-dates in multiple publications, Hertzog advises keeping the design consistent with postcards or invitations to ensure that persons recognize the information is for the same event.

Source: Stephanie Hertzog, Director, Public Relations, Providence Hospital, Washington, DC. Phone (202) 269-7021. E-mail: shertzog@provhosp.org

This save-the-date reminder was featured in the Winter 2008 community newsletter for Providence Hospital (Washington, DC).

Year in Review Can Boost Morale, Show Value

In large organizations, there is always a lot going on — much of it newsworthy. To help recap and focus that positive coverage, compile a year-in-review feature that you share on your website and/or in print form.

Nicole Pitaniello, assistant vice president for public relations, Albany Medical Center (Albany, NY) says its year-in-review piece is a source of pride for the organization. The piece, she says, reminds people of the great things that happened at the center over the year while underscoring how valuable their publicity is to the institution.

"People sometimes comment that we don't do enough paid advertising," Pitaniello says. "The year-in-review feature is a way to help offset that argument. We are able to show that the communications department yields benefits for the hospital.

"By placing these in-depth stories in a variety of local media, we're getting way more space and credibility than we could ever afford through traditional advertising. We're getting double and triple the coverage this way. We're also getting third-party credibility because it's an outside source saying the work we do is valued. It's not just coming from us."

In addition, Pitaniello says, "It's a nice reminder for people to keep us in the loop about what is happening, so we have the stories to tell."

Source: Nicole Pitaniello, Assistant Vice President for Public Relations, Albany Medical Center, Albany, NY. Phone (518) 262-3421. E-mail: PitaniN@mail.amc.edu. Website: www.amc.edu/pr/yearinreview/year_in_review.html

Donor-centric Catalog Lets Prospects Browse Giving Choices

Are you looking for a one-stop resource for donors and development staff alike? Consider the giving catalog produced by the University of Pittsburgh (Pittsburgh, PA).

Jasmine Hoffman, manager of public relations in institutional advancement, says that since its inception in December 2008, the online catalog has received more than 1,200 unique page views and is the seventh most-visited page on the site.

Hoffman says the most interesting analysis though is in the page's bounce rate.

"The bounce rate measures the number of people who leave the site after viewing only one page," she says. "Eighty-seven percent of the users who visit the giving catalog are navigating through multiple pages in the catalog. The giving catalog is providing prospective donors with quality information about giving while they research their philanthropic interests."

So how does the giving catalog work?

Prospective donors visit the website at www.giveto.pitt.edu/catalog/index.asp through an easy link on the home page of the university's website. There they are able to research giving opportunities through four filters: university priorities, dollar amount, key words and build your own gift. Once they have reviewed their options, they can be linked directly to a development officer.

Here's a great way to encourage would-be donors to browse giving options on your website.

"Inquiries go directly to the development officer who is fundraising for that particular initiative. The site also allows development staff to quickly send information to prospective donors. For instance, if a donor wants more information about a Student Resources Fund in the School of Arts and Sciences, the development officer can quickly e-mail an information sheet about that gift to a donor," says Hoffman.

Their primary goal in developing the catalog, Hoffman says, was to serve as an information source for donors and development officers. "It's doing that and more. Feedback so far has been positive, with users finding the catalog intuitive and easy to use."

Source: Jasmine Hoffman, Manager of Public Relations in Institutional Advancement, University of Pittsburgh, Pittsburgh, PA. Phone (412) 624-5847. E-mail: jasmine.hoffman@ia.pitt.edu

---

Three Tools to Evaluate Giving Catalogs

Jasmine Hoffman, manager of public relations in institutional advancement, University of Pittsburgh (Pittsburgh, PA) says their online giving catalog has been a hit with alumni, prospective donors and development officers alike. How did they know that would be the case when they were developing the catalog? They did thorough research and utilized Web analytics. Hoffman offers the following tips to make sure similar tools work effectively for you:

1. **Do your research first.** Hoffman says focus groups and online surveys told them that many of their donors visit the university's website to explore giving opportunities before completing an online gift or contacting the development office. This led them to believe the catalog would be a natural extension of that need for research and information.

2. **Understand how your donors think.** A comprehensive card sort analysis helped them understand how donors organize giving opportunities and terms on the website. Hoffman says, "The card sort analysis helped us identify the categories and terminology to use in the giving catalog. We wanted the giving catalog to be donor-centric so we thought it was appropriate to organize it according to the responses from the card sort analysis."

3. **Use the technology available.** Hoffman says Web analytics have allowed them to see that the students' category is the most successful area within the giving catalog and that most Web visitors are navigating to that section of the catalog first. Analytics have also allowed them to know how many unique page views the site has received and how many people leave the website after viewing only one page. All of this information allows them to tweak the catalog to make it more user friendly.

Online giving catalogs offer a creative way for would-be donors to identify funding opportunities that suit their interests.

Nonprofit Publications What You Need to Know to Create Winning Publications

OUTSOURCING: WRITING, PHOTOGRAPHY, DESIGN AND PRODUCTION AND MORE

Should you enlist the help of an advertising firm or do it yourself? Does the job require the expertise of a professional photographer or can you turn to a volunteer with photograph experience? Do you have time to write it yourself, or would it make more sense to turn the job over to a freelance writer? These are the kinds of questions that any communications office needs to answer at varying times throughout the year.

Pros and Cons of Outsourcing Publications

Staff with The Girl Scouts of Central Texas (Austin, TX) have outsourced production of a 124-page program guide, Possibilities, to a local design firm since 2005. Haila Yates, communications director, shares pros and cons of doing so.

Positive points of outsourcing:

✓ Aside from content development, the process is hands-off, freeing up valuable staff time. "We print Possibilities two times a year, and if we didn't outsource it, it would take up at least six months of our design specialist's time," says Yates. "The firm does the layout and formatting, and prepares print-ready files that they then supply to our printer."

✓ The final product is polished and professional, attracting readers. "We end up with a professional, appealing publication that our membership enjoys and greatly relies on," says Yates. "It would be almost impossible to create this publication without outsourcing it."

Negative points of outsourcing:

✓ Deadlines imposed by external sources may be difficult to manage. "Multiple staff members supply content for the publication, and we must stick to a strict content deadline to accommodate the designer's schedule," says Yates.

✓ The editing process may become lengthy and complicated. "Edits are extensive and time-consuming both for us to communicate accurately to the designer and then for the designer to make," says Yates. "Then we have to check to make sure the edits were made correctly. There is much room for miscommunication in this process."

When determining whether to outsource a project, Yates advises, list pros and cons before and during a project to ensure you are choosing the best option for your organization. In her organization's case, "I would definitely say that the pros outweigh the cons."

Source: Haila Yates, Communications Director, Girl Scouts of Central Texas, Austin, TX. Phone (800) 733-0011. E-mail: HailaY@gsctx.org

Before outsourcing a publication, make a list of the pros and cons.

Interview Firms Before Outsourcing

Are you considering outsourcing brochures, website design or other materials? Jon Snavely, vice president, sales and marketing, Snavely Associates (Park City, UT), and Susan Burlingame, director, communications/senior writer, Snavely Associates (State College, PA), recommends asking prospective firms:

- What is your experience? (For example, if you are a university, can the firm you choose navigate the world of academia?)

- Who is on your team?

- Whom will I be working with directly?

- What is the process like?

- Do you enjoy what you do?

Sources: Jonathan Snavely, Vice President, Sales & Marketing; Susan Burlingame, Director, Communications/Senior Writer, Snavely Associates, Park City, UT. Phone (435) 615-7979. Website: www.snavelyassociates.com

Ask these five questions of firms before deciding who should get your publications business.

Outsourcing Campaign Brochure Proves Successful

When a project is beyond your in-house expertise, look to hire an outside firm.

As staff at Iowa State University Foundation (Ames, IA) began preparing for a major campaign in 2005, they also began looking for a firm to assist with campaign communications, says Ann Wilson, senior director of communications.

The goal of the campaign, which ends Dec. 31, 2010, is $800 million, with $550 million in gifts and commitments received to date — with the help of a campaign case brochure and other campaign materials professionally prepared by Snavely Associates (Park City, UT and State College, PA).

"Snavely Associates was chosen for their experience, price, philosophy — one price quoted up front and no charges for changes along the way; and size of the firm — not too big; not too small," says Wilson.

Foundation staff were in constant contact with Snavely staff, says Wilson: "I probably talked to Jon Snavely every day, if not more, during the two years, either by e-mail or phone."

The centerpiece of the foundation's campaign was a 30-page campaign case brochure (shown in part at right) developed over 18 months.

"Snavely provided the overall design, but we gave lots of input and went through several rounds of revisions," says Wilson, noting that they were particularly detail oriented on this project, created to be hand-delivered to high-end donors foundation development officers.

In preparation for designing the brochure, Snavely staff spoke with donors, administrators, faculty and students to find out why people loved ISU and why they would want to donate, Wilson says. The brochure includes a letter from ISU's president, student testimonials, features on main areas the foundation is raising funds for, photos, a letter from the volunteer campaign chair, and a page detailing why and how donors can give to the campaign.

The brochure and other printed pieces that came out of the partnership could not have been accomplished without the help of an outside agency, Wilson says. "Our staff was involved in so many details and projects getting ready for our public campaign launch, not to mention all our daily operational work, that we could have never found time to produce these materials.

"Also, it was helpful to have an outside perspective and to work with a firm that had created these types of materials for other clients and could advise us on trends, what works, etc.," she adds.

"The brochure is successful because it captures the essence of Iowa State and only Iowa State," says Susan Burlingame, director, communications/senior writer, Snavely Associates. "It does a beautiful job of connecting their historic mission to their mission for the future, and it makes the case for their campaign alone. The color, writing and feel ... represent and reflect Iowa State values, Iowa State ambitions, Iowa State accomplishments — no one else's."

When looking for a firm that will suit your outsourcing needs, Wilson advises, make sure it has the staff to handle your project. Are costs all-inclusive or will you be billed for changes, phone calls, etc.? Does your management team feel comfortable with the firm you've selected?

Finally, knowing all costs up front and staying within budget are vital components of a successful partnership, says Wilson. "Make sure you know and understand all of the estimates and make sure you stay within your budget. A higher-cost project doesn't always mean a better/higher quality product."

For more about ISU Foundation's campaign materials prepared by Snavely Associates, go to: http://www.snavelyassociates.com/e_isu.html

Source: Ann Wilson, Senior Director of Communications, Iowa State University Foundation, Ames, IA. Phone (515) 294-9608. E-mail: awilson@foundation.iastate.edu. Website: www.withprideandpurpose.org Susan Burlingame, Director, Communications/Senior Writer, Snavely Associates, State College, PA. Phone (814) 234-3672. Website: www.snavelyassociates.com

New Brochure Is Child's Play for Discovery Center

Everybody loves a good game. That belief led staff at the Albany Pine Bush Discovery Center (Albany, NY) to partner with the East Coast-based marketing communications firm Eric Mower and Associates for their new discovery center's brochure.

The result was a four-color, fold out brochure designed as a Seek & Find in the Pines game board. People can use coins as game pieces, moving around the brochure board and answering questions relative to the Pine Bush Preserve.

Wendy Borden, communications and outreach director, Albany Pine Bush Preserve Commission (Albany, NY), says the two-sided, informative, fun-to-play format serves as a general-use brochure for the discovery center, one of just 20 inland pine barren environments in the world.

Borden says they receive much positive feedback on the game concept, which has been a cost-effective way to attract families who live and travel throughout the region.

Being able to create a brochure using colorful graphics instead of photos also helped overcome the biggest challenge planners faced in designing the brochure prior to completion of the discovery center — finding usable photos or other artwork, she says. Instead of photos, the board game became the publication's focal point, with the organization's stock photos of the ecosystem scattered around the game board.

Content not available in this edition

The brochure, shown in part at the left, provides visitors before they visit the discovery center the opportunity to learn more about what they might see or experience there.

Source: Wendy Borden, Communications and Outreach Director, Albany Pine Bush Discovery Center, Albany, NY. Phone (518) 456-0655. E-mail: wborden@tnc.org

Give Freelance Photographers Clear Expectations

Hiring a freelance photographer can provide your organization with valuable photos for your marketing materials without costing your organization a lot of manpower.

"When using outside resources for images, I've had good luck with following basic guidelines," says Marc Sheehan, editor, Ferris State University's (Big Rapids, MI) alumni magazine. "Use your network of contacts for freelance recommendations. Digital technology has made it easier to view a freelance photographer's work. It's good if they have a website with previous work and even better if they have the technology to post thumbnail versions of photos you can purchase from the photo shoot they do for you."

Clearly communicating your needs is imperative to creating a positive working relationship with any freelance photographer. "Be clear with the freelancer what it is you want. It helps if you can send them the text that will accompany the image. As in so many circumstances, failure to communicate is the cause of headaches that could have been avoided. If all else fails, negotiate a kill fee that fits your budget to avoid any problems should the image prove unusable," says Sheehan.

Source: Marc Sheehan, Editorial Services Coordinator, Ferris State University, Big Rapids, MI. Phone (231) 591-2376. E-mail: sheehanm@ferris.edu

When Hiring a Freelance Writer....

Once you have found a potential freelance writer, what comes next?

Samples and references are the two most important things to check, says Linda Olson, executive director of communications, Eastern University (St. Davids, PA). "Credentials are nice but those alone are not a reliable guide," she says. "What you need to see are actual writing samples. These should be diverse enough to give you a good idea about the writer's ability."

"You need to feel confident about their work and their understanding of your topic," says Lisa Maggart, marketing consultant, Arketi Group (Atlanta, GA). "It's also important to make sure you have a comfortable working connection with this person. Remember, while this may be a single project, you'll be working with them to communicate your message to your audience."

What questions are important to ask when you're interviewing a potential freelancer? Questions may include:

✓ How many years have you been writing?

✓ Have you worked in an agency environment or just corporate? Agency experience enables a person to work fast, learn an industry quickly and meet multiple deadlines.

✓ What industries do you know well? What topics are you most passionate about?

✓ Have you won any awards for your writing? This isn't a necessity but it's always a plus to hire a writer who has won recognition for their work.

✓ What are your experiences in interviewing and message development?

✓ What vehicles have you written for (e.g., newsletters, websites, brochures, press releases, industry white papers, etc.)?

✓ How much do you charge? Writers typically charge by the hour or project. If billing is by project, how many rounds of revisions does that allow for?

✓ Can you provide client references? Be sure to contact them to ask about the writer's work style and other issues. Questions to ask references include: Are they reliable? Do they meet deadlines? Is their work quality consistent? Do they stay within the agreed-upon budget? Will they represent the organization well when they make one-on-one contacts?

Consider using the freelancer you hire again for various projects.

Source: Lisa Maggart, Marketing Consultant, Arketi Group, Atlanta, GA. Phone (404) 929-0091. E-mail: Lmaggart@yahoo.com
Linda Olson, Executive Director of Communications, Eastern University, Davids, PA. Phone (610) 341-5930. E-mail: lolson@eastern.edu

Be sure to follow these next steps before making a final decision on who to hire as a freelance writer.

Find Freelance Writers

Looking for a freelancer? Search for freelance writers on craigslist — www.craigslist.org. Craigslist consists of local classifieds and forums for 450 cities worldwide.

Susan Tellem, president and CEO, Tellem Worldwide Inc. (Los Angeles, CA), locates freelancers on craigslist.

"Employers can post a listing, which costs about $25 in some cities and is free in others," Tellem says. "Or you can review the posts from writers who are looking for work."

Another advantage for employers, Tellem says, is they can sort through a blind response box, which means the freelancer doesn't know your organization information. Craigslist also makes it easier to reach freelancers in your geographical area.

Other ways to find freelancers include: ask colleagues in your industry for recommendations; contact a professional communications organization, such as the Public Relations Society of America (www.prsa.org); participate in online discussion groups relevant to the topic on which the writer will be working; take note of bylines in related magazines, books and newspapers; and do a Google search for exactly what you want (e.g., press release writer).

Source: Susan Tellem, President and CEO, Tellem Worldwide Inc., Century City, CA. Phone (310) 479-6111. E-mail: stellem@tellem.com

Successful Collaborations Require Planning, Hard Work

Many organizations use an outside marketing firm when developing or redesigning key communications materials. While this can be a worthwhile collaboration, be sure you know your expectations and your limits before you sign a contract.

Content not available in this edition

Content not available in this edition

Staff with Furman University (Greenville, SC) worked with an outside public relations firm to redesign key communications pieces, including its website, top and alumni magazine, above.

Staff with Furman University (Greenville, SC) have worked with the same outside firm, Stamats (Cedar Rapids, IA), for eight years.

The marketing and advertising firm has helped create an updated set of integrated marketing materials for the university, including its admissions magazine and integrated Internet microsite, says Gregory Carroll, Furman's vice president for marketing and public relations.

"It has been a very cooperative and collegial relationship," Carroll says of the partnership. "We came to them with a lot of ideas of things we had seen and things we wanted to accomplish and asked them to put their expertise to that."

Carroll shares advice for nonprofit communicators planning a similar collaboration:

- **Choose the right firm.** If you evaluate the vendor as if you were hiring an onsite employee, you are more likely to get a good match. Also talk to their other clients about their experience working with them.

- **Dream big.** The best examples of what you want to do might come from the real world of business and entertainment. Collect what you like and what you think might work for you and share it with your vendor.

- **Create a plan and stick to it.** Make sure you put down in writing exactly what you expect to happen and exactly what resources you have to bring to the project. The better the planning, the better off you'll be after the project closes.

- **Control your budget.** Change orders mount up and you have to be aware of that so as not to be surprised when the bills come. In addition, what appears to be a bargain may not be, so don't always go for the low bid or cheapest option.

- **Keep communication lines open.** Be forthcoming and honest in how you deal with the firm on a day-to-day basis and at the end of projects. If you don't like something, say so. Realize and accept that the firm must be able to do the same.

- **Don't stop working on the project.** Plan on supporting the project after it is delivered. Most of these projects do not have a crisp beginning and ending, but there is maintenance that continues after the vendor leaves you, so plan for it.

Source: Gregory Carroll, Vice President for Marketing and Public Relations, Furman University, Greenville, SC. Phone (864) 294-3108. Website: www.furman.edu

Use Consistent Branding Message Throughout Your Communications Tools

After a successful launch of their organization's first-ever website, officials with Chelsea Revere Winthrop Elder Services (Chelsea, MA) decided they wanted to reflect a consistent branding and marketing message throughout their communications pieces.

To help accomplish this, Carol Nestor, director of community services, turned to IlluminAge Communication Partners (Seattle, WA) — designers of the nonprofit's new website — to expand the website design to their marketing and outreach brochures.

"Our objective was to replace outdated materials with more professional-looking materials with the ultimate goal of attracting more clients," says Nestor.

IlluminAge staff took elements that would easily translate from Web to print (e.g., the color palette, graphics style and images) and carried them over to the brochure's design, making the two communications tools look consistent.

"A consistent look and feel enforces a unified message," says Connie Parsons, IlluminAge marketing director. "An organization can spend less time explaining who they are, what they do and why they do it if their message is consistent."

After receiving positive feedback following the website launch in January 2008, Nestor and staff put two brochures into circulation five months later. Each brochure promotes a different agency service or program while encouraging the community to support the organization. The brochures are given to professionals, older adults and caregivers in the communities the agency serves. Plans are to produce two additional brochures in the coming months.

While it's too early to measure the effectiveness of the brochures, Nestor says the website redesign has brought in $1,000 in unsolicited gifts. Total cost to brand the website and brochures, $3,000.

Source: Carol Nestor, Director of Community Services, Chelsea Revere Winthrop Elder Services, Chelsea, MA. Phone (617) 884-2500. E-mail: clnestor@crwelderservices.org
Connie Parsons, Marketing Director, IlluminAge Communication Partners, Seattle, WA. Phone (800) 448-5213. E-mail: connie@illuminage.com

Colors, photos, fonts and other key design elements remain consistent throughout the marketing pieces for Chelsea Revere Winthrop Elder Services (Chelsea, MA), including its Web page, top right, and brochures.

Select Elements Carefully When Creating Consistent Brand Message

Connie Parsons, marketing director, IlluminAge Communication Partners (Seattle, WA), says usability is key in choosing which elements stay and which change when transitioning from Web to print design or vice versa.

To create a consistent brand message, no matter what format you are working with, Parsons recommends considering these elements:

- **Colors.** Colors play an integral part in creating a consistent brand message," she says. "A consistent color palette and strong use of logo can make an organization quickly recognizable by the community."

- **Images.** "Strong use of images also enforces the brand image," says Parsons. While images may change more frequently than colors, it's important to use photos with the same feeling and message.

- **Font.** Parsons says a good designer will recognize what fonts work well on the Web and what ones work well in print. While sans serif fonts enhance usability on a site, a serif font is easier to read in print. Also consider font size when transitioning your message from Web to print. In the case of Chelsea Revere Winthrop Elder Services branding, the font size for the Web, while adjustable, began at 10 point. However for the brochures the designer chose a font that is readable by most people at 12 point.

Nonprofit Publications What You Need to Know to Create Winning Publications

COST-SAVING IDEAS

As you know, throwing more money at publications doesn't necessarily make them any better. In fact, sometimes less is more when it comes to the design and look of a particular publication. Especially in light of the current economy, the following cost-saving ideas will help to stretch your publications budget and help you to work smarter.

Make Publications Look More Polished for Less

Being good stewards of donors' money means constantly looking for ways to minimize expenses. One way to do so is to choose the least expensive method possible to create printed materials without significantly compromising quality.

Follow these tips to help keep printing costs down:

Paper:

Check out these ideas for cutting back on publication expense without cutting back on their look.

✓ **Ask for house stock.** If you request a specific type of paper not in stock, printers have to order way more than you need for the job, passing that expense on to you.

✓ **Add the words "or equal to" the paper line in your bid.** This gives the printer latitude to substitute a similar stock paper at a lower price.

✓ **Ask for donated paper.** The printer may have overage from other jobs that will work, so be prepared to be flexible in your paper color and type choices.

✓ **Ask about current trends in the field.** Currently, coated stocks are about the same price as uncoated and foreign papers are as cheap as domestics. Both of these choices will help your piece look more polished at a lower price.

Color:

✓ **What's the difference?** You may be surprised to find that without bleeds, four color printing can be affordable and effective for certain showcase pieces.

✓ **Stay away from custom colors** which, like bleeds, can add considerable cost.

Setup:

✓ **Make sure the file is correct.** The job file should be ready to go to press when you deliver it to the printer. Additional edits after that point can prove costly.

✓ **Consider size.** Try to stick to 8 1/2 X 11-inch or multiples of that standard size (half or quarter sheets of an 8 1/2 X 11-inch sheet).

✓ **Utilize waste.** If you must use an odd paper size, see if you can use the waste in some way, such as note pads, business cards or other small jobs that could be printed on the edges of the paper, which normally would be trimmed and tossed.

✓ **Order more than you need.** Ordering in volume will save you money.

Source: Tony Saccone, Sales Representative, Lane Press, Albany, NY. Phone (518) 438-7834.

Four Tips for Getting the Most Bang for Your Buck in Print

Creating and printing direct mail appeals can eat a huge hole in your development budget.

Shaké Sulikyan, director, annual giving and alumnae relations, Pine Manor College (Chestnut Hill, MA), offers four ideas to reduce the cost for such pieces:

1. Test all mail packages before implementing them across the board with all constituents.

2. Have visual arts or graphic design students design pieces, reaching out to your board and constituent network to find qualified persons. You can also challenge design students from a local college or technical institute to come up with a winning design.

3. Use online printers such as www.vistaprint.com and overnightprints.com.

Here are four ways to get a better handle on your direct mail costs.

4. Look for willing hands to help with assembly. Who among your network might be able to help with such a project? Volunteers? A scout troop? Church youth looking for community service hours? Keep a list of such projects handy so you are ready to match willing workers with needed tasks.

Source: Shaké Sulikyan, Director, Annual Giving and Alumnae Relations, Pine Manor College, Chestnut Hill, MA. Phone (617) 731-7099. E-mail: ssulikyan@hotmail.com

Consider Paperless Options to Save Expenses, Resources

A lot of talk has been given to the paperless office, though now that seems more a lofty aspiration than an achievable goal. Many nonprofits don't have the resources or the time to update their computer systems to the level necessary to sustain that goal.

That doesn't mean there aren't ways to make your office greener, starting with the hard considerations about which things are worth committing to paper. When deciding what and how much to print, ask yourself the following questions:

- **Is this piece absolutely necessary?** The hard part about this question is being honest with your answer. If you feel like you can't be brutally honest because you are too close to your work, ask a sampling of your constituents.

- **What sort of response have we gotten from this piece in the past?** If the answer is little or none, you may want to consider doing away with the piece.

- **Can we get the same outcome for less** (less paper, less waste, less money)? Is it possible to send a letter that can be duplicated in-house directing people to the same information on your website (e.g., a letter thanking donors for their support that directs them to a PDF file of your annual report online)?

- **Who is on our mailing list?** Does the volunteer bulletin really need to go to the people who work once a year at your holiday booth? Does the newsletter need to go to every donor or can you set a benchmark, only sending it to those who donate $100 per year or more?

Taking these simple steps will not only help put you on the road to a greener future, they will also save your organization money and that's news everyone wants to hear!

It pays to ask yourself these questions before moving ahead with a printed publication.

Save Money on Direct Mail Pieces

Kathy Connolly, vice president of sales and marketing, The MailWorks (Albany, NY), says the following tips, many of which should be considered in the planning stages, can shrink your mailing costs:

- ❑ **Think machinable.** Anything that must be done by human hands costs more, including hand matching of addresses on inner pieces and outer envelopes, folding or sorting. Make sure envelopes you use can go through mailing and sorting machines. Also make sure that there are no bright colors in the address area that can make it non-machinable. Postal surcharges apply to pieces that cannot go through machines.

- ❑ **Apply white space.** Make sure to leave a 2 X 4-inch white space for address area.

- ❑ **Don't be a square.** A square design requires a 21-cent surcharge. Consider folding 8 1/2 X 11-inch pieces to 5 1/2 X 8 1/2-inches to cut postage in half. For postcards, avoid a line down the middle, which limits bar code use and can increase postage.

Finally, Connolly says, have your mail house or provider review your design files before you print to avoid unpleasant budget surprises waiting for you at the post office.

Source: Kathy Connolly, Vice President, Sales and Marketing, The MailWorks, Albany, NY. Phone (518) 435-9300. E-mail: kconnolly@themailworks.com

Here are some additional ideas on how you can save money with direct mail pieces.

Understand Incremental CPMs

Sometimes it just makes good sense to print extra copies of a brochure or annual report or some other publication. That's when it's important to analyze the CPMs: cost per thousand impressions.

When you make a decision to increase a printing job by 1,000, 5,000 or more copies for additional distribution, it's important to look at this as a variable cost. That's the cost of the additional quantity to print and not the average cost per copy. This will give you a true snapshot of what your returns need to be to justify the cost of printing additional copies of your publication.

Advice for Crafting Creative, Cost-effective Brochures

When you sort your own mail, you likely use your visual and tactile senses as much as you use critical thinking skills: bills in one stack, flimsy flyers, junk mail and advertising in another, and eye-catching designs printed on attractive paper stock with personal mail.

With a little planning and creativity, you can help ensure the brochures and other materials you send donors, constituents, prospective donors and other target audiences make it to the keep stack.

If your brochures will be used in racks or accompanied by letters, know that attractive presentation invites the recipient to take a closer look and read the message.

A few basic design tips and printing ideas will help you plan brochures that stand out from other reading materials and save you money as well:

It's one thing to be creative. It's another to be both creative and cost effective. Here are some ways to do just that.

- **Make two colors of ink look like more.** Most commercial printers have two-color presses. This means it costs little more for you to use two ink colors instead of one, because most presses print both colors in a single pass. Extra cost of a second color is usually a press plate and a negative. If you choose ink colors like red and blue, an overlay of the two colors together will create purple, whereas yellow and blue will make a green and red and yellow will combine to give you orange as a third design choice. Use of an overlay of the two base colors as an accent can give added dimension to your brochure for very little money.

- **One ink color may be enough.** Even if your brochure budget or your printed quantity is too small to justify commercial printing, you can create a professional appearance with black or one other color on its own. Include screened or reversed areas to highlight visuals or special text. Experiment with your computer's graphics program to see if it includes special effects such as drop shadows behind text boxes or fonts, outlined type for headlines or titles and curved or shaped text. Print your original copy in black ink and take it to your copy center to run in one of their standard colors.

- **Have fun with your paper stock.** No matter how many (or how few) colors of ink you use, you can add color through your paper stock choices. Call a representative from one or more of your local paper companies and ask for swatch books of stocks that meet your needs. If your organization orders lots of printing and paper, the rep may even bring you a cabinet of all of the house sheets available. Most brands and types of paper come in a variety of color choices, textures, weights and laser-compatible surfaces. Many office supply stores carry a good selection of papers that can be bought in quantities of 100 to 500 sheets. Examples include parchments, linens and pebble textures.

- **Experiment with simple folding techniques.** While choosing a readily available paper size like 81/2 X 11- or 11 X 14-inch keeps your costs low, you may make unexpected design choices to add to the piece's appeal. For example, design your graphics to show when folded at a certain angle or fold a standard size vertically rather than horizontally. Before you lock yourself into an unproven design, realize that getting too complicated can be expensive or cause difficulty for your printer, so asking for advice first can avoid most concerns. Your printer can be a valuable source of ideas for easy but unique folds or die cuts. Even if others have used the same technique, your design, colors and papers will make yours look new.

- **Ask for cost differences between different weights of the same paper stock.** If you have a choice between a 100# text or an 80# cover of the same paper, the latter is likely to be heavier. If a heavier weight is desirable, ask your printer if the stock is heavy enough to require scoring first. The scores (made on the fold) will help heavier papers fold smoothly and evenly. A lighter weight of the stock may not need scoring before passing through the printer's folding machine and save money. You decide where the extra costs are warranted.

Save brochures that attract your attention and use them for design ideas. Visit with your printer or paper house representative to see how you can achieve a similar effect with minimal resources. Keep in mind that the paper you use is your artistic canvas, and a high-quality stock may cost only slightly more than standard fare.

Recycling Ideas: Don't Let Extra Issues Go to Waste

With all you invest in printed communications pieces, the last place they should end up is uncirculated and in the trash.

Next time you have extra publications (e.g., brochures, annual reports, newsletters) lying around, try one or more of these creative ideas to circulate them before they become outdated:

1. Keep your reception desk, waiting rooms, lunchroom and other public areas well stocked with the publications, topped with a small Help Yourself! card.

2. Add display pockets to your public elevator area and keep filled with brochures, newsletters and other materials for your visitors to read.

3. Fold materials to fit in business-sized envelopes and deliver to departments in your organization that send communications to new contacts, e.g., billing, new donors, persons seeking additional information about your programs, etc.

4. Bring extras to board and staff meetings and ask the attendees to take and share with their co-workers, neighbors, etc.

5. Provide the materials to your local Chamber of Commerce, Realtor board or other Welcome Wagon-type organization that has contact with community newcomers.

6. Mail or have volunteers deliver pieces to medical, dental and other offices, senior service agencies and other places with waiting areas. Get the business's OK to place the materials in a waiting room or reception desk before doing so

Save on Printing Costs

- Printing a three-color job requires two passes through a two-color press, or a more expensive four-color press. Either way, that third color costs you. To save money, use screens or overprints to give the impression of a third color with only two ink colors.

Strapped for Time, Cash or Looking for High Impact? Send World's Smallest Newsletter

A multi-page newsletter isn't the only way to get your message across.

What if a special event is in a month and your quarterly newsletter isn't due for six weeks? Or your budget is dwindling down? Or you just want to try something new and fresh?

Send a simple postcard newsletter.

"Postcard newsletters are a great way to deliver small bits of information," says Heidi Richards, author and marketing strategist based in Mirimar, FL. "You can send your message quickly, inexpensively and frequently; if you send it regularly, people will start looking forward to receiving it."

Since a postcard newsletter is the Reader's Digest of a traditional four- to eight-page newsletter, Richards says, think condensed. For example, three ideas with high impact that people will remember far outweigh a list of 10 tips.

Design the postcard like a newsletter with columns, headlines and short, snappy sentences or bullet points. Tips, facts and quotations work well.

As for e-mailed postcards versus those sent by regular mail, choose the latter, Richards says. "While e-mail postcards may be easier to produce, they are also easier to delete and I just don't think they are that personal. Besides, you don't need a computer to read regular postcards — anyone can get your message."

Content not available in this edition

Quick to create and inexpensive to send, a postcard newsletter can pack lots of information in a small space.

Cut Printing and Postage Costs by Using Postcards

Finding new ways to cut costs is important to any organization. Here's how one nonprofit uses postcards preprinted with color photos and the organization's logo to inform community members and supporters about important announcements or events.

"As an in-house marketing group, we often field requests from internal departments who have little or no printing budgets but need announcements or invitations," says Kristi Eaves-McLennan, director of marketing and communications, Meredith College (Raleigh, NC). "To help remedy these requests, we've begun working with our printers to print 4 X 6-inch postcards (featuring images from around campus). This gives us a variety of postcards featuring a four-color image and our corporate logo to offer to departments to meet their needs at little cost to them."

Printing a large amount of postcards in advance — and doing so in conjunction with another four-color press job — saves considerable time and money.

Consider using postcards with preprinted photos and your logo as an economical way to communicate with targeted groups.

"We are able to print four or five different postcards along with the cover of one of our recruitment publications," Eaves-McLennan says. "This has given us a stock of 35,000 postcards (7,000 of each design) at virtually no cost. This would cost upwards of $5,000 if we were to print them as a separate print job."

Departments needing postcards for announcements or event invitations simply request the amount needed and have the appropriate information printed on back.

"We usually ask for one to two weeks' notice," she says, "but we store the postcards in-house and can produce them more quickly if needed. For some departments who use the postcards on a regular basis, we've set up a pre-approved template system with a local printer that allows for a quicker turnaround time."

All cards contain a photo of the Meredith campus along with the college logo. At least one of the available designs will feature the college tagline: "I Believe...that a good life starts here. At Meredith."

Source: Kristi Eaves-McLennan, Director of Marketing and Communications, Meredith College, Raleigh, NC. Phone (919) 760-8455. E-mail: eavesk@meredith.edu

Here are a few of the preprinted, full-color postcard designs that Meredith College marketing and communications staff keep on hand for college-related activities. The back side is blank and can be personalized as needed.

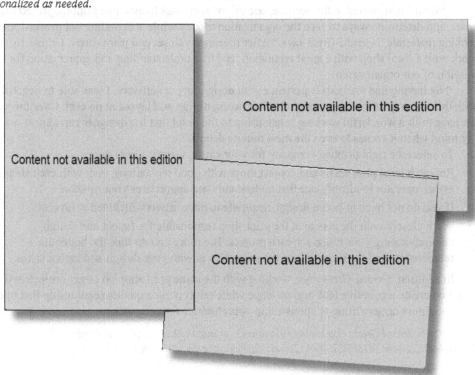

Dos and Don'ts When Seeking Free Printing

Printing costs can take a big chunk of your budget. Not surprisingly, printers often receive requests for donated services. By necessity, they've become practiced at saying no diplomatically, especially to elaborate publications.

However, many printers are willing to donate services to nonprofits that approach them in a reasonable, businesslike manner. To secure an in-kind gift from your printer for your next project:

1. **Do remember the printer's costs.** These include paper; envelopes; ink; labor; press and bindery time; and delivery. Instead of asking for free services, ask the printer to consider completing the job for you at cost.

2. **Do provide paper or envelopes.** Some printers gladly donate the press time and labor for a good cause if you send the materials. Stay with standard dimensions.

3. **Do use available supplies.** Your local paper company also receives more requests for donations than it can honor. Increase your chances of getting a yes by agreeing to take a house sheet bought in bulk at a low price or a discontinued style.

4. **Don't use high-pressure tactics.** Your nonprofit may pay a favorite printer a fair price for most projects, but don't try to use that to leverage a freebie. You don't give them business, you patronize them because their prices and quality meet your needs. Never ask a new printer for a donation by dangling the possibility of future paid business before them.

5. **Do be familiar with a company's donation policies.** Large printing companies may prefer to be paid for work they do for your organization and give a sizable cash donation instead.

6. **Do provide camera-ready art.** Give the printer your job ready to be shot as a negative and made into a printing plate. A printer who has agreed to donate services will be unpleasantly surprised if your job requires extensive repair or typesetting. Talk in advance about what they need to do the job effectively.

To improve the odds of securing in-kind services from your printer, turn to these six approaches

Choose a Printing Company That Fits Budget, Mission

Finding a printing company that is both affordable and intuitive of your needs will facilitate a long-lasting working relationship and hopefully result in stellar collateral materials.

Deb Gerard-Gress, community relations coordinator, Hospice of North Central Ohio (Ashland, OH), relies heavily on outside printing firms to produce materials.

"When I first started at the hospice, one of my goals was to evaluate printing projects and costs, and determine ways to save the organization money while still putting out professional-looking materials," Gerard-Gress says. "After meeting with several print shops, I chose to work with a local shop with a great reputation, and true understanding and appreciation for the mission of our organization.

"Not having had previous experience with design/layout software, I was able to negotiate with the sales rep at the shop to include all artwork, design and layout at no cost. Over the years, we have built a wonderful working relationship to the point that the designer can almost read my mind when it comes to even the most minute details."

To select the right printing company for your cause, Gerard-Gress says:

- Research local print shops and contact those with good reputations; visit with each shop's owner/operator to identify one that understands and appreciates your mission.

- If you do not have in-house design, negotiate to have artwork included at no cost.

- Work closely with the person at the print shop responsible for layout and design, communicating your vision for each project. The more you do this, the better the relationship, and the more in tune the print shop is with your design and layout tastes.

In addition, Gerard-Gress says, working with the same print shop on larger projects will help you create a cohesive look and message while reinforcing a quality relationship that opens doors to future underwriting or sponsorship opportunities for your cause.

Source: Deb Gerard-Gress, Community Relations Coordinator, Hospice of North Central Ohio, Ashland, OH. Phone (419) 289-4844. E-mail: dlg@hospiceofnorthcentralohio.org

Consider Digital Offset Printing

Want full-color dynamic design without paying a fortune? Try digital printing.

Laura Rogers, art director at Dandelion Design (Rensselaer, NY), cites additional ways digital offset printing can benefit your print needs and your bottom line:

- ✓ Allowing you to customize individual pieces to customer needs, offering the option of different data on each sheet.
- ✓ Dramatically reducing turnaround time compared to traditional methods.
- ✓ Offering ability to print on a wide variety of papers, including textured and translucent.
- ✓ Creating unlimited color opportunities and color vibrancy, mimicking offset quality from a digital press.
- ✓ Clear, durable coating that enhances photos and protects mailings.
- ✓ Short-run printing of offset quality in quantities as few as one.
- ✓ Glossing unit that will coat gloss stock with a laminate-like finish.

Before you decide to design and print in two colors because of cost issues, Rogers suggests checking with your local four-color printer to see if they have a digital press. Many medium to large printers are now offering this printing option.

Source: Laura Rogers, Art Director, Dandelion Design, Rensselaer, NY. Phone (518) 283-9474. E-mail: lea@dandesign.com

Digital offset printing can help your bottom line.

Get Donors to Underwrite Publications Costs

Looking to cut back on expenses and raise more money at the same time? Get businesses and/or individuals to underwrite your nonprofit's publications.

Begin by developing a menu that lists each of your nonprofit's publications along with sponsorship prices and brief descriptions of each. (See generic example, below.)

You may choose to begin with a limited number of publication sponsorship opportunities and then keep expanding your list in subsequent years.

In addition, you may wish to list sponsor benefits associated with each publication or address those perks as you meet with would-be donors. Minimally, each publication would say: "This publication made possible through the generosity of..."

This method of raising gifts is more attractive than simply asking for an outright gift to support general operations. Donors can see exactly how their gifts help your nonprofit and enjoy the reminder each time they receive a copy of the publication they support.

This partial list of publication sponsorship opportunities illustrates how you might create a menu suited to your nonprofit's publications.

Consider getting some of your key publications underwritten by sponsors

XYZ Hospital Foundation Publication Sponsorship Opportunities

To help direct more of the hospital's limited resources toward valuable patient services, we invite you to underwrite one or more of our hospital's regularly printed publications. Each sponsorship opportunity carries certain benefits that will be shared with interested parties:

- ❑ **Heartbeat Magazine (3 Times per Year)**   **Cost: $9,000**
  This award-winning magazine is distributed to everyone on our mailing list (former patients, clients, community leaders, area businesses and more).

- ❑ **Annual Giving Brochure (Yearly)**   **Cost: $900**
  This publication serves as the development office's primary tool for inviting annual gift support. Sponsorship of this publication helps the hospital foundation broaden its base of annual support.

- ❑ **Planned Giving Newsletter (Quarterly)**   **Cost: $1,800**
  This valuable resource helps to nurture planned gifts (bequests, annuities and more) that will ensure our hospital's future. In the past year alone, the hospital received $650,000 in bequests.

Nonprofit Publications: What You Need to Know to Create Winning Publications.
Edited by Scott C. Stevenson.
© 2010 Stevenson, Inc. Published 2010 by Stevenson, Inc.

How do you know if a particular publication is really accomplishing its intended purpose? In fact, how do you know your publications even get read? The articles found in this chapter will help you to analyze and evaluate your publications' overall effectiveness.

Measure the Impact of Your Communications Efforts

Measuring the impact a communications piece or project has on its intended audience is a crucial part of the process that will help improve your future communications.

"Measurement begins with properly setting the goals and expectations of a communications project in the beginning," says Meredith Elkins, senior communications and information officer, Eurasia Foundation (Washington, DC). "Knowing what you're trying to accomplish and what success will look like is critical to knowing when you've achieved it."

Once you establish specific goals, create a set of activities to achieve those goals.

"Producing a press release is not a goal, it's an activity," says Elkins. "Why did you produce the press release? To get the word out about your mission, event, new president, etc. How do you know if you succeeded? A way to measure that is with traditional marketing measurements; press coverage is measured in the number of placements plus the number of your messages contained within each placement."

She offers another example of creating activities to establish goals. "Let's say you redesigned your website to make it more user friendly. When you announce the redesign, you'll want to track audience response, so set up your Web traffic tracker to capture how people move through the site and how much time they spend on each page."

The same strategies can be applied to most communications projects, Elkins says, stressing that knowing what your expectations are before you begin is vital to being able to gauge the success of the project.

Source: Meredith Elkins, Senior Communications and Information Officer, Eurasia Foundation, Washington, DC. Phone (202) 234-7370. E-mail: eurasia@eurasia.org

> *Measuring a publication's impact should begin with setting goals and expectations*

Offer Incentives to Increase Survey Participation

Use incentives as a motivational tool when promoting your surveys.

The Bayer Center for Nonprofit Management at Robert Morris University (Pittsburgh, PA) has offered incentives to motivate target audiences to participate since its first survey in 2000, says Jeffrey Forster, director of technology services and research.

Survey participants have been offered at least two perks: A copy of the survey report and discount coupons for Bayer Center classes worth up to $100.

"A copy of the survey report makes sense because it creates a feedback loop; you tell us where you stand and we'll tell you where the sector stands," says Forster. "The coupon is a win-win because we like to have people come to our training, too."

Participants in the 2008 survey had a chance to win a digital video camera. The winner's name was announced in the organization's e-newsletter and at local events.

Forster says the incentives encourage participation, as shown by the steady increase in numbers, from 172 persons in 2000 to 329 in 2008.

He offers these tips for organizations considering offering survey incentives:

> *Looking for ways to improve your survey's response rate? Consider these ideas*

- **Offer incentives your audience wants.** If unsure what to offer, conduct a formal or informal survey.

- **Offer incentives you can afford.** Forster says the cost of the video camera plus printing and distributing copies of the survey report was around $1,300.

- **Make sure your target audience knows about the incentives.** Use e-mail, direct mail, information on your website and other communications tools.

Source: Jeffrey Forster, Director of Technology Services and Research, Bayer Center for Nonprofit Management, Robert Morris University, Pittsburgh, PA. Phone (412) 397-6005.

Survey Readers to Gather Valuable Feedback

Reader surveys can provide valuable feedback that can help shape your publications.

Staff at Salve Regina University (Newport, RI) began using online reader surveys for their Report from Newport magazine in 2003. Originally created as a printed piece that polled alumni for feedback, the survey (www.salve.edu/news/rfn/rfn-survey.cfm) is now posted in the online newsroom of the university's website. The brief survey:

✓ Asks readers to rank in order from one to six a list of topics they would like to see covered in the magazine.

✓ Provides space for readers to fill in other topic ideas in which they are interested.

✓ Share general feedback and comments.

✓ Asks alumni to share their news and updates so that their information can be included in the class notes section of the magazine.

The survey is evolving, says Deb Herz, managing editor of publications, university relations and advancement, and developer of the survey questions.

"I'd like to include a section on the survey where readers can write letters to the editor, giving them more of an opportunity to critique the articles and comment on the stories," says Herz. "This would create a forum for feedback and open dialogue, which could lead to editorial improvement."

Developed with help from the university's webmaster, the survey took about a week to create, including drafting the survey, creating and posting the online version. The survey cost nothing beyond staff time to create.

Information submitted through the surveys is stored in the university's database and is used to inspire new topics and features, says Matt Boxler, public information officer, university relations and advancement.

Four Steps to Online Survey Success

Looking to create a reader survey? Matt Boxler, public information officer, Salve Regina University (Newport, RI), offers four tips for reader survey success:

1. Make your surveys multi-dimensional.

2. Welcome constructive criticism.

3. Offer readers incentives for participating in the survey as a means to motivate them and to get a wider cross section.

4. Structure questions to have a balance of open-ended and close-ended responses.

"Submission for news and events are printed in the magazine and sometimes, after a review from the editorial board, we'll get a larger feature story out of a submission," Boxler says. "One example is a submission received from 1965 Salve Regina graduate Ellen Roney Hughes, who reported that she was curator for a national exhibit on sports memorabilia at the Smithsonian. It turned into a more comprehensive feature on her hobby and her career, written by a student, which was in response to another feedback item submitted by a reader who said they'd like to see more stories written by students."

When the survey was first launched, the university received roughly 12 completed surveys each week. Since that time the number of responses has decreased.

"The pace has slowed, but it is understandable as the university now implements several methods for communicating with its readers to garner editorial content for the magazine," says Boxler. "Examples include the office of alumni, parents and friends' use of Harris Connect, an online community through which readers can submit their own personal news, career news, upload photos, etc. Additionally, the development office's phonathon callers ask for updated news and events that can be included in the magazine."

While they are not currently promoting the online survey, Boxler says plans are to do so in a variety of ways.

"When the survey is reworked and improved, we plan to direct readers to it via the magazine itself, the university website and by establishing links on the emerging social media electronic avenues," says Boxler.

Sources: Matt Boxler, Public Information Officer; Deb Herz, Managing Editor of Publications; University Relations and Advancement, Salve Regina University, Newport, RI. Phone (401) 341-2156 (Boxler) or (401) 847-6650 (Herz). E-mail: boxlerm@salve.edu or herzd@salve.edu

Survey Helps Define Readers' Interests, Gives Readers a Voice

Butler University (Indianapolis, IN) just concluded its five-year capital campaign, ButlerRising, with 20,000 donors making gifts and pledges of nearly $154 million — $28 million above goal. But no time for laurel resting, because last fall, Butler leadership implemented its 2009-2014 strategic plan, Dare to Make a Difference.

One tool for defining the challenges for the new plan and overall university marketing is a reader survey conducted via Butler Magazine, produced three times a year at 45,000 copies for students, alumni, parents and friends of the university, including donors and potential donors.

Sally Cutler, director of print marketing and communications, and editor of the magazine, says that in developing the concise, two-page survey, Butler's university relations team had three primary objectives:

1. To determine which aspects of the magazine are most read.

2. To learn what topics about Butler are of greatest interest.

3. To draw a detailed picture of readers' perceptions of the university.

The extended university relations group intends to implement the survey as a living resource for strategic and tactical marketing direction, Cutler says. They started looking to survey responses for guidance just two days post-deadline. At a crossroads in an ongoing discussion of where and how to list donors — and needing to make a timely decision — they culled responses to the question "How would you prefer to read the Honor Roll of donors traditionally included in the winter issue of Butler Magazine?"

In creating the survey, staff drew on several organizations' models, with the highly survey-focused University of Evansville (Evansville, IN) as a key source.

Butler Magazine has surveyed readers before, but Cutler says not for a long time. Her group now plans to conduct more surveys, she says, noting that in today's communications environment, audience participation is the expected norm, and without a two-way conversation, organizations jeopardize their credibility. Giving readership a voice is imperative in creating the sense of community essential in fundraising and all nonprofit support activities.

Source: Sally Cutler, Director of Print Marketing and Communications, Butler University, Indianapolis, IN.
Phone (317) 940-9742.
E-mail: scutler@butler.edu

Shown in part here, this two-page survey, featured in Butler Magazine, a publication for students, alumni, parents, donors and friends of Butler University (Indianapolis, IN), gave its readers a voice as to what they would like to see in magazine content.

By completing the survey by **June 15**, you will be entered into a drawing for a Butler gear gift basket. Thank you so much for your time and support of Butler University — *we appreciate and value your input.*

Tell us about yourself *(mark all that apply)*
☐ Butler University alumnus or former student
  Year of graduation _____
☐ Parent of Butler University student
☐ Butler University faculty or staff member
☐ Other (fill in) _____

What topics do you like (or would you like) to read about in *Butler Magazine?*
(mark all that apply)
☐ Academic initiatives
☐ Alumni events and opportunities for involvement
☐ Campus/student life
☐ Donor news and giving to the University
☐ Faculty news
☐ General University news
☐ Individual alumni

What types of articles are you most likely to read?
(mark all that apply)
☐ Brief profiles   ☐ News items
☐ Full-length features   ☐ Opinion/commentary
☐ Other _____

How would you prefer to read the Honor Roll of Donors traditionally included in the winter issue of *Butler Magazine?*
☐ Included in the winter issue as in the past
☐ As a separate issue but packaged with *Butler Magazine*
☐ Online
☐ I don't read the Honor Roll of Donors
☐ Other _____

How much time do you spend reading each issue?
☐ 15-30 minutes
☐ 30-60 minutes
☐ More than one hour
☐ Less than 15 minutes
☐ Don't read it

In general, do you read the magazine:
☐ Within a few days of its arrival
☐ Within two weeks
☐ Within a month
☐ On and off over several weeks and months

Which departments in this issue of the magazine did you read?

Alumni News
☐ Read   ☐ Skimmed   ☐ Skipped
Bulldog Bulletin
☐ Read   ☐ Skimmed   ☐ Skipped
Class Acts
☐ Read   ☐ Skimmed   ☐ Skipped
From the President
☐ Read   ☐ Skimmed   ☐ Skipped
46th and Sunset
☐ Read   ☐ Skimmed   ☐ Skipped

I am most likely to read something in the magazine because of *(check all that apply)*
☐ Familiarity with the individuals or work featured in a story
☐ Subject matter that interests me
☐ Interest in issues concerning the University
☐ I read everything in the magazine

Which of the following adjectives would you use to describe the magazine? *(check all that apply)*
☐ Informative
☐ Intelligent
☐ Irrelevant
☐ Pride-building
☐ Unappealing
☐ Useful

Which of the following actions have you taken as a result of reading or looking through the magazine? *(mark all that apply)*
☐ Saved an article or issue for future reference
☐ Discussed or sent an article to someone else
☐ Renewed contact with a fellow alumnus
☐ Decided to become more active with the University
  (join an alumni chapter, contribute financially or other)

Rate the overall quality of *Butler Magazine*

Overall appearance
☐ Excellent ☐ Good ☐ Average ☐ Poor ☐ No opinion
Readability
☐ Excellent ☐ Good ☐ Average ☐ Poor ☐ No opinion
Quality of writing
☐ Excellent ☐ Good ☐ Average ☐ Poor ☐ No opinion
Timeliness/relevance of content
☐ Excellent ☐ Good ☐ Average ☐ Poor ☐ No opinion

Focus Groups Contribute Valuable Ideas, Feedback

Staff at Binghamton University (Binghamton, NY) use student focus groups to review many of their print publications and gather feedback on images and content, says Gregory Delviscio, director of publications.

In March 2008 the university held an on-campus focus group to gain insight from current students on a series of residential life postcards, says Delviscio. "The goal of each of the postcards was to pique student interest in the university's unique residential communities, as well as to encourage them to sign up early for housing."

The focus group lasted two hours and included refreshments. The students were given a list of questions to discuss and their responses were recorded to review later, he says. "Each postcard was unveiled separately and the students were also each given a hardcopy print to look at and react to. We then posed the survey questions and I documented each person's response."

Consider focus groups as one way to get valuable feedback on particular publications.

The eight students, from sophomores to seniors, had lived on campus their entire experience at Binghamton, says Delviscio. "The focus group provided us with a range of rich insight into what students felt were the more popular and exciting programs offered in the residential communities (and) helped us craft some of the wording and assist in developing eye-catching headlines to fit a younger audience."

Delviscio worked with residential life staff to identify students from all three class years. Other methods to solicit participants, include inviting volunteers, supporters and community members through mass mailings, mass e-mails or online posts.

Offering a small payment, event tickets, refreshments or lunch to participate may increase turnout, says Delviscio. "Cash works the best when you want a focus group to show up, but short of that food also works well, especially with a younger crowd."

Source: Gregory Delviscio, Director of Publications, Binghamton University, Binghamton, NY.

Take Steps to Maximize Focus Groups

Binghamton University (Binghamton, NY) assembled a student focus group to offer input on the design of postcards such as the one shown here. To make the most of a focus group, here is advice from Gregory Delviscio, director of publications:

- Have someone in charge who can keep the group focused on the questions. Opinions tend to fly in these meetings, so they must be kept on track.

- Don't let one person dominate the group.

- Choose someone with no emotional attachment to the project to run the meeting. Make sure the person in charge has a thick skin. The process shouldn't turn into a defense of the project. It's to get honest feedback from fresh eyes.

- Understand the group dynamic; call on people to seek independent responses.

Content not available in this edition

Content not available in this edition

Graphic Guidelines Help Establish University Uniformity

Establishing and sending a consistent image reinforces a nonprofit's credibility.

At Baylor University (Waco, TX), marketing officials noticed nearly every school, department or program within the university was being marketed in ways inconsistent with Baylor's trademarks. So they took action, developing and adopting a plan in 2004 to establish uniformity in the university's branding efforts.

Paul Carr, director of marketing information, says the president's office authorized a cross-functional committee representing academic, athletic and administrative areas to establish Baylor's graphics standards program.

"Prior to our first committee meeting, our marketing team assembled samples of the multiple ways our brand was being used and misused by internal constituents across the university. We also looked at what other institutions had done with their graphic standards," says Carr.

"These two sets of materials were extremely valuable for participants who were unfamiliar with the problem we were discussing," he says. "First, the materials served as visual aids that clarified our purpose in meeting. Second, we showed committee members that peer institutions had graphic standards and that we were not alone in our efforts."

Taking more than a year to develop, the program is a set of guidelines that focus on the use of Baylor trademarks by departments in marketing the university. The program identifies guidelines for use of the institutional mark, university seal, family of athletic or spirit marks, business cards and stationery.

Carr says color restrictions are also detailed in the program, requiring any two-color university marks to use the university's official colors, which are identified using Pantone® Matching System numbers.

Staff and faculty received e-mails about the new standards and a link to the website (www.baylor.edu/graphics/). The licensing and trademark office holds training classes on campus twice a year to explain proper use of the marks. Licensing, marketing and legal counsel participate.

"Consistency and the way these icons are presented are very important to building brand awareness and maintaining a connection with our various audiences," says Carr. "The standards enable us to avoid changes based on personal opinion rather than policy."

Source: Paul Carr, Director of Marketing Information, Baylor University, Waco, TX. Phone (254) 710-4693.
E-mail: Paul_Carr@baylor.edu

Advice for Creating a Graphics Standards Program

Staff at Baylor University (Waco, TX) have a graphic standards program in place that helps guarantee all entities within the university adhere to its branding standards. Paul Carr, director of marketing information, shares five tips for creating a graphic standards program:

1. **Establish the importance and credibility of the effort.** In Baylor's case, that authority came from the university president, who appointed members to the committee charged with establishing the graphic standards with the expectation they would report to him. The president also formally signed and adopted the graphic standards as policy.

2. **Have broad participation in the process.** Carr says all members of the Baylor committee — which included representatives from academics, athletics, development, marketing, student life, printing, the licensing office and general counsel's office — provided valuable input that shaped the final policy.

3. **Start with the right frame of mind.** While marketing staff knew the university needed graphic standards, Carr says it wasn't their goal to bring in a particular set of standards and have the committee approve them. "We wanted to discuss the different types of standards and for the committee as a whole to decide what they thought would be best for university," he says. "Using this participatory approach, we ended up with an amazing level of buy-in to the end product."

4. **Continue to meet even after project is complete.** Even after five years of the standards being in place, Carr says the committee's key players — marketing, creative services, general counsel, licensing, printing and athletics — routinely e-mail, call or meet to discuss issues or concerns.

5. **Allow for flexibility.** Because rules cannot be written to cover every conceivable issue, Carr says there are times a request comes across that is not specifically addressed in the standards. He then reminds the individual of the university's intent of the program. If the request meets the intent of the standards, then it usually is allowed.

Nonprofit Publications: What You Need to Know to Create Winning Publications.
Edited by Scott C. Stevenson.
© 2010 Stevenson, Inc. Published 2010 by Stevenson, Inc.

Nonprofit Publications What You Need to Know to Create Winning Publications

PUBLICATIONS IDEAS WORTH CONSIDERING

Want to learn what's working for other nonprofit organizations when it comes to publications? We have identified several winning ideas and success stories that you will want to consider as you evaluate your own publications needs and opportunities.

Highlight Impressive Facts With a Top 10 List

Don't overcomplicate things. Next time you're looking to share interesting facts or reasons to support a specific cause, consider a Top 10 List.

That technique worked well several years ago for Middle Tennessee State University (MTSU), Murfreesboro, TN, where officials created a publication highlighting the top 10 facts people might not know about MTSU.

The list pulled key information into one easy-to-read, easy-to-share publication, says F. Douglas Williams, executive director, marketing and communications.

"These facts are well-known strengths of the university," says Williams.

While the Top 10 publication is no longer produced, the list is included in MTSU's visitors guide and also referred to throughout its facts and figures guide. The university produces and distributes 5,000 copies of each publication every year.

"When we first developed the Top 10 list publication, we wanted to include facts that people might not be aware of and that gave people a good feel for MTSU," says Williams. "We also included things unique to MTSU, such as signature programs in aerospace, recording industry and the concrete management program."

He and other staff decided to create the list after being inspired by late-night talk show host David Letterman's popular Top 10 list. If your organization already has an extensive facts sheet, he advises pulling the most interesting, newsworthy and/or appealing top 10 and creating and sharing them in list format.

Be sure to keep the information fresh, says Williams, noting that MTSU's 2008 Visitors Guide contains an updated Top 10 list.

"Each year we look at the list and reevaluate it," he says. "The marketing office gets input from other people on campus, most notably the publications and graphics office." The input gathered is informal, he says, and while the list generally remains the same from year to year, updates and changes are made as needed.

Williams says that a list of this kind is appealing to readers because it is easier to remember and repeat than reading this information in a longer narrative format.

*Source: F. Douglas.
Williams, Executive
Director, Marketing and
Communications, Middle
Tennessee State University,
Murfreesboro, TN.
Phone (615) 898-2919.
E-mail: fdwillia@mtsu.edu*

Middle Tennessee State University's Top 10 List:

1. MTSU is a destination school and is the No. 1 choice of undergraduates in the state of Tennessee.

2. One of the finest teacher preparation institutions in the southeast, MTSU produces 26 percent of the state's certified teachers — by far the most of any university in Tennessee.

3. The Center for Popular Music is nationally recognized as a repository of music, and has one of the largest sheet music collections in the country. It was listed as one of the top 100 things to visit in Tennessee in the 20th century by the *Tennessean.*

4. A member of the Sun Belt Conference MTSU, competes at the highest level in all 17 sports. Many Blue Raiders have gone on to success in both the Olympics and the professional ranks.

5. Students enjoy numerous extracurricular activities, with more than 190 student organizations, including honor societies, service clubs and an active Greek system of fraternities and sororities.

6. The Honors College, with its prestigious Buchanan Fellowships—the highest academic scholarships awarded at MTSU, provides talented students the atmosphere of a small select college nestled within a major university.

7. Ph.D programs in English, economics, human performance and public history have been called programs of the highest quality and the programs in economics and public history are unique in Tennessee.

8. Nationally recognized programs in aerospace, recording industry and concrete management attract students from around the world.

9. MTSU initiated and now sponsors the Tennessee Teachers Hall of Fame, a statewide entity which recognizes the lifelong achievements of those in the teaching profession.

10. Our safe and friendly environment has a diverse student body which is 54 percent female, 12 percent minority, and with students from around the world.

Enrich Your Outreach Materials With a Top 10 List

"Top 10 lists can be great tools when used correctly," says Suzanne Lee, communications and marketing director, Care and Share Food Bank for Southern Colorado (Colorado Springs, CO). "They not only spice up regular copy or news releases, but also draw the journalist's attention to the many different facets of your organization, as well as how it relates to their general readership."

"We are all very passionate about our organizations and the work we do, but it's important to show journalists how their readers are intrinsically connected to the many different facets the nonprofit covers," says Lee. "Top 10 lists can be great tools, as long as they're not blatantly self-serving."

The food bank created a useful list, Top 10 Ways to Save Money on the Family Groceries, which includes tips such as:

- Visit your local farmer's market. The food is usually local, inexpensive and healthy.
- Shop with your grocer's customer appreciation card.
- Buy in bulk whenever possible, but make sure you're still getting a good value. Bulk packaging can be deceptive.

"If you do choose to drive people to your website (with the list), make sure you have the content listed clearly on the homepage," says Lee. "There's nothing more frustrating to a consumer or potential donor when they visit a website (than finding) the information that's been promised them isn't there."

Top 10 lists can be used in brochures and other printed materials to illustrate key points about your organization or to highlight specific programs.

"I would suggest not to overuse them or they'll lose their edge," says Lee. "They should be used to provide readers with additional tips and hints to increase their quality of life or to learn more about what your nonprofit is doing in the community, not to invite them to your next fundraiser."

Source: Suzanne Lee, Communications and Marketing Director, Care and Share Food Bank for Southern Colorado, Colorado Springs, CO. Phone (719) 528-1247, ext. 219.

Top 10 lists add a unique element to your outreach materials and can serve as an eye-catching way to convey important information.

Facts-at-a-glance Handout Makes Great Leave-behind

What eye-catching, message-embracing materials do you leave with persons who may not be very familiar with your organization?

Could you be overwhelming them with too much, too soon?

It's easy to inundate constituents with so much information that they end up reviewing none of it. That's why your nonprofit's arsenal of handouts should include a concisely written, easy-to-read brochure of facts about your nonprofit's purpose, programs and those you serve.

This collection of facts will help set the stage for establishing relationships with key players such as customers, donors, would-be donors and volunteers.

Depending on the amount of information you wish to share, this information can be printed on a one-page sheet, in the form of a bookmark, a multi-panel brochure or any number of formats. Just remember to keep it concise. Boil down what you have to offer into a handful of key facts.

Use this checklist of key information found on such introductory pieces to craft your own:

Your arsenal of handouts should include a concisely written, easy-to-read brochure of facts

- ❑ Year founded and by whom.
- ❑ Mission statement.
- ❑ List of services provided.
- ❑ Number of clients served.
- ❑ Yearly budget amount.
- ❑ Client profile summary.
- ❑ Number of employees.
- ❑ Annual payroll.
- ❑ Distinguishing characteristics.
- ❑ Calendar of events.
- ❑ Testimonials.
- ❑ Summary of future plans.
- ❑ Key contact information.
- ❑ Where to go for more information.
- ❑ Map of facilities and locations.
- ❑ Description of outstanding facilities and equipment.

Produce Materials in Two Languages

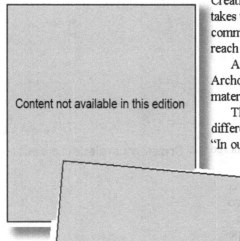

Creating accurate and worthwhile materials in more than one language takes tremendous effort. For some organizations, reaching out to a community not fluent in English is critical to achieve their mission and reach those in need of their services.

According to Linda-Ann Gabriela Salas, public affairs officer, Archdiocese of Denver (Denver, CO), the biggest challenges of producing materials in two languages are cost, time, space and manpower.

The motivation for providing materials in multiple languages may be different for each nonprofit but the challenges and benefits are similar. "In our situation, it's not only beneficial, it's crucial to the success of our Hispanic Ministry and Centro San Juan Diego. If we didn't provide Spanish services, many Hispanics would fall through the cracks. We offer a myriad of social and spiritual services and programs in Spanish. We feel integration starts first in meeting the immigrants where they are in their own language and then helping them integrate into the larger community by learning and using the English language," Salas says.

When creating materials in more than one language, Salas says, "Know your audience and their education level. Make sure your translator translates for those you are trying to reach. For example, if your audience is Mexican and you have a Peruvian translator, the translation will not be accurate."

Source: Linda-Ann Gabriela Salas, Public Affairs Officer, Archdiocese of Denver, Denver, CO. E-mail: linda-ann.salas@archden.org

A sampling of materials produced in multiple languages by the Archdiocese of Denver.

Keep Those (Thank-you) Cards and Letters Coming!

For nonprofits dependent on donations, saying thanks is an important skill to master. And saying thanks in a personal way can be especially meaningful in this era where e-mail and technology are taking the place of human touch.

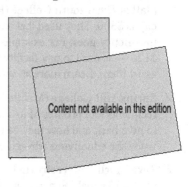

Set an example within your communications department of how to thank donors or volunteers. Model the art of saying thanks by issuing thank-you notes to staff and volunteers who assist you in various ways. Address the note to an entire department and jot on the envelope, please post and share with your staff.

Recognize the importance of saying thank-you in a personal way.

Develop a simple, inexpensive thank-you card and envelope using your organization's logo. Bundle the cards in sets of 25 and bring the bundles to your next management meeting. Share them with your organization's administration and management, along with a cover sheet that outlines ideas for sending a thank-you note.

Here's the kicker, tell the persons to whom you distribute the cards that you'll bring bundles of thank-you notes to meetings every three months — and that you expect them to have exhausted their existing supply by then!

Let staff know that you have extra thank-you notes in your department for them to pick up should they need to replenish their supply before the next meeting.

Door Hangers Get Your Message to Home, Business Owners

For an inexpensive, in-your-face awareness tool, consider door hangers.

Whether laminated or card stock, printed in one color in-house or sent to a printing company for full-color brilliance, door hangers get the attention of your audience the minute they walk through the door.

Door hangers are the perfect communications tool for number of situations.

For instance, door hangers offer:

1. **Targeted distribution** — If you're planning a fund-raising walk or a community fair, recruit volunteers to adorn doors throughout the walk or fair area to notify residents of the opportunity and encourage them to attend.

2. **Focused messages** — Offering a limited space, door hangers force you to get your message across in just a few words, which is always good experience! Remember to include your Web address, phone number and/or a call-to-action that motivates recipients to do something.

3. **A chance to raise awareness** — You're virtually guaranteed that recipients will find a door hanger unusual enough to take a closer look. So if you need to get a message out fast to a specific area — such as persons in an apartment complex or student dorm — a door hanger may be just the tool to use.

Content not available in this edition

Why Give? See How Six Nonprofits Encourage Donors to Give

Looking for inspiration and fresh ideas to better connect potential givers with opportunities to give? Here are examples of how other nonprofits are finding creative ways to answer the question, "Why give?"

- ✓ Staff at **Dartmouth College** (Hanover, NH) determined that the cost per student per day is $300. They used that amount to illustrate on a pie chart (shown at right) where that money goes. For example, the pie chart shows that a large chunk of that $300 — $126 — is used to pay faculty who love to teach undergraduates and the staff who assist them. Learn more at: www.dartmouth.edu/~alfund/why_give/index.html

- ✓ **Spring Hill College** (Mobile, AL) uses quotes and photos of its college scholarship recipients and profiles of its donors to show prospective donors why it is important to give back and how they can make a difference with their gifts. See details at: www.shc.edu/giving/why-give

- ✓ **Texas Tech University** (Lubbock, TX) recognizes that everyone has their own reasons for making a gift, and lists some of those: "You want to return the favor;" "It's good business." For more info: www.texastech.edu/development/whygive/

- ✓ **MADRE** (New York, NY) shows fiscal responsibility with graphic charts showing who gives to their organization (individuals, institutional funders and others) how those donations are used. See charts at: www.madre.org/index.php?s=3&b=11

- ✓ **Children's Hospital Boston** (Boston, MA) shares success stories through profiles and photos of the children the hospital has helped. Check it out at: http://giving.childrenshospital.org/NetCommunity/Page.aspx?pid=225

- ✓ **Rainforest Action Network** (San Francisco, CA) created a video illustrating its mission and sharing success stories to encourage donors to "Become Part of the Solution." Watch the video at: http://ran.org/give/why_give/

Content not available in this edition

Partnership May Be Key to Creating New Publication

Thinking of creating a new publication?

Consider partnering with another like-minded organization to split your costs while doubling your potential audience.

Before launching the magazine, Cities Mean Business (shown at right), staff with the Municipal Association of South Carolina (MASC) of Columbia, SC spent two years researching possible publishing and distribution options.

"Our goal of this external publication was to integrate our message of strong cities into existing venues where our target audiences would see it," says Reba Campbell, deputy executive director.

MASC staff considered several statewide organizations as potential partners before finding their current partner, a statewide business journal entitled SC Biz.

There can be multiple advantages to partnering with another organization on a publication.

Content not available in this edition

"We had been working with them both on the news and advertising fronts for a year and quickly realized their audience was our audience," says Campbell. "We worked with them to have our 16-page magazine inserted into their existing magazine two times annually. Our staff served as the editorial staff identifying stories, writers and direction. The SC Biz staff took our design direction and developed the layout so our insert would have the same look and feel as their magazine.

"Working with the SC Biz staff was a pleasure because they contributed a design expertise that we don't have on our staff," she says.

Campbell says the magazine was created as part of a larger campaign to bring attention to individual communities in South Carolina and highlight the state's economic success.

"The feature stories and columns reflect the ongoing messages that we are trying to communicate in this campaign," she says. "Since the magazine is part of a larger campaign, identifying topics and messages for the publication was easy."

To make the project a success, Campbell says, "we used the four steps of research, planning, implementation and evaluation. It is especially important not to overlook the research phase. Had we gone with our initial plan of publishing a magazine ourselves, we would have missed out on many of the benefits of partnering with SC Biz.

"The cost in terms of staff time and outsourcing probably would have been about the same as what we paid SC Biz for the design, printing and space in the magazine, which totaled around $10,000."

Source: Reba Campbell, Deputy Executive Director, Municipal Association of South Carolina, Columbia, SC. Phone (803) 799-9574. E-mail: RCampbell@masc.sc

Newsletters Can Do the Pitch for You

Looking for a passive but consistent way to regularly pitch stories to the news media? Add your media contacts to your newsletter mailing list.

Whether reporters receive your newsletter in their e-mail or in their morning mail delivery, a quick review of your publication might be just the spark they need to contact you about pursuing a story triggered by something in the publication.

To make a reporter's job even easier, attach a paper clipped or self-stick note to a story you believe would be of particular interest to the recipient.

While this outreach method should never be a substitute for personal contact, it is a great way to get your information in newspersons' hands and increase the odds of getting your organization's name in the news.

Partnerships Enrich Advocacy Efforts, Communications

Teaming up with other nonprofits can provide you with the talent, credibility and resources necessary to increase the reach and impact of your advocacy efforts.

In July 2006, the Firelight Foundation (Santa Cruz, CA) launched a 32-page publication, "From Faith to Action," endorsed by 21 other organizations. The publication was developed as an advocacy tool aimed at promoting family- and community-based responses for the care and support of children affected by AIDS and to reduce the number of children left without care or placed in orphanages.

Publication Emphasizes Investing in Community-based Solutions

Zanele Sibanda Knight, interim director of programs, says they sought out organizations that understood the need for support of community-based groups responding to the challenge of HIV/AIDS in their communities. Rather than create a mailing or formal campaign, they relied on established relationships and referrals from other organizations and contacts.

Four organizations provided financial support for the project, with the foundation covering more than half the $75,000 cost. Two foundation staff members and a member of the foundation advisory board wrote the publication, with partner organizations including UNICEF contributing ideas. Representatives of most organizations reviewed drafts and provided valuable feedback throughout the process.

The publication includes photos, strategies, stories, quotes, resources and lists all partner organizations involved in the project.

"The key message of the publication is that investing in community-based approaches enables children to be provided and cared for within families," says Sibanda Knight. "The approach we took to this document was to provide examples of a range of strategies used by grassroots organizations to ensure that children remain in family care. The strategies are based on the 12 principles to guide programming for orphans and vulnerable children, which were developed through a consultative process facilitated by UNICEF."

Partner Organizations Help Distribute Collaborative Publication

Each partner organization helped distribute copies of the publication through its own networks. The foundation has made the publication available for download on its website and has utilized it at conferences and speaking engagements.

Two versions of the publication were printed: 30,000 copies of the full-length 32-page issue, and 50,000 copies of a six-page summary. The publication is also available in PDF format at: www.firelightfoundation. org/publication-02.php.

Collaboration Results in Far-flung Visibility

The foundation's visibility has grown substantially because of the publication.

"We are now seen in the field as an authority on getting resources to grassroots organizations that support family- and community-based care for vulnerable children," says Sibanda Knight. "The publication has reached far-flung places that we didn't anticipate, and raised awareness of the foundation as a leader on the support for the care of orphans and vulnerable children."

Source: Zanele Sibanda Knight, Interim Director of Programs, Firelight Foundation, Santa Cruz, CA. Phone (831) 429-8750. Website: www.firelightfoundation.org

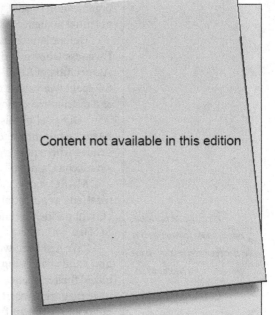

Content not available in this edition

Collaborative Publication Draws Strong Online Interest

"From Faith to Action," a publication that is a collaborative effort of 22 organizations coordinated by the Firelight Foundation (Santa Cruz, CA), spread the word about the value of family- and community-based responses for children affected by AIDS.

Firelight Foundation officials say that in the first year after they put the publication on their website, they saw website traffic jump from 12,000 to 21,000 hits per week, which they credit directly to downloads of the publication.

Pull Out Creative Stops When Designing Event Invitations

Invitations to your organization's events need not be costly to be effective, memorable and capable of bringing out the attendees.

Here are some ideas to get you started or inspire more ideas for your creative team:

✓ **Share business card-sized invitations**. The who, what, when, where and why of most events can fit on one or two sides of a typical business card, especially if an event is open to the public and formal mailing lists aren't needed. Leave stacks at cooperating stores, distribute at networking events and ask volunteers to hand out.

✓ **Carefully evaluate needs**. Will your invitation design have equal impact with just one or two colors? A well-executed graphic with an attractive layout will look great in black or grayscale, and markedly decrease production costs.

✓ **Stick it!** Shop the marketplace for bright adhesive stickers in interesting shapes and design your basic invitation to accommodate them in the design theme. Besides using them on the invitation itself, you can add them to the mailing envelope and response cards.

✓ **Use surplus materials in your inventory**. Take a tip from Scarlett O'Hara, who wore a stylish gown made from curtains. Leftover blank envelopes and outdated letterhead trimmed to size can be a blank canvas for your invitation, even if they are different colors or stock.

✓ **Offer plantable, printable paper**. Attractive seeded papers, party favors, place cards and even confetti are now available from online retailers and specialty stores. When planted, your event materials can grow into flowers and other foliage.

✓ **Look online for ready-made cards**. Sourcing artwork and design on invitation websites helps you obtain professional-looking results and saves money and time. Dozens of online retailers offer broad selections of stock images with themes for total invitation packages that are printed and shipped to you within a week or two. Some also will provide matching artwork for e-cards.

✓ **Vary your materials**. Consider integrating into your invitation design a swatch of colorful fabric, twine, a scented die-cut flower, a spiced tea bag or other small item that fits your event theme. Appropriately used, this adds color, interest and context.

Here are some creative ideas to consider when producing invitations

Content not available in this edition

Bookmarks Find Their Place In Marketing Package

Looking for an extra piece to add to your marketing package — one that serves a purpose so people will actually use it?

Karen Readey, director of communications, Midland School (Los Olivos, CA) says bookmarks worked for her organization.

"We wanted something that provided information about the school, but that was also practical," Readey says. "Since we're a school and that involves a lot of reading assignments, a bookmark made perfect sense. Plus, we list authors who graduated from Midland, along with their publications on one side of the bookmarks."

Readey says they sent the bookmarks (shown to the left) to the school's entire mailing list and take them to all conference events or school fairs they attend.

Source: Karen Readey, Director of Communications, Midland School, Los Olivos, CA 93441. Phone (805) 688-5114. E-mail: kreadey@midland-school.org

Campaign Helps Launch Compelling Marketing Piece

Officials with the Kappa Alpha Order Educational Foundation (Lexington, VA) developed a six-page, full-color brochure to highlight naming opportunities for their capital campaign.

The brochure outlines size and type of gifts that would receive naming opportunities and recognition donors would receive. Naming opportunities are divided into giving levels based on the foundation's giving clubs. Gifts of $500,000 or more, for example, are listed in The Robert E. Lee Circle section, and gifts of $250,000 to $499,999, in the George C. Marshall Society section.

Larry Stanton Wiese, executive director of the foundation, says brochures that feature naming opportunities should list all naming opportunities and amounts and pledge fulfillment terms, such as if estate gifts can be used to reserve a naming opportunity. Offer a variety of options, as some donors prefer typical bricks and mortar naming opportunities, while others prefer a named scholarship or an endowment/program naming opportunity.

To share the funding opportunities with more potential donors, foundation officials posted a downloadable PDF online, featured the information in their quarterly magazine and foundation annual report, mailed the brochure to donors and prospects, and gave it to donors and prospects in face-to-face meetings.

Source: Larry Stanton Wiese, Executive Director, Kappa Alpha Order and the Kappa Alpha Order Educational Foundation, Lexington, VA. Phone (540) 463-1865, ext. 2001.
E-mail: lswiese@ka-order.org

Any campaign publication should include a list of gift opportunities with corresponding costs.

Content not available in this edition

Pages from Kappa Alpha Order Educational Foundation (Lexington, VA) brochure highlight named giving options that match its giving clubs.

Content not available in this edition

Content not available in this edition

Top 10 List Can Support Asks for Campaign

In Arlington, TX, the community really does own the hospital. More than 50 years ago, residents pooled their money to build the original 75-bed Arlington Memorial Hospital.

Now, hospital leaders believe the community will be just as generous in contributing to their first-ever capital campaign, It's My Hospital, Keeping Our Promise.

The campaign has a goal of $10 million.

One way they are encouraging donors is through an online list called the Top 10 Reasons to Give, shown below and online (www.texashealth.org).

John Hyde, director of development, says the list was developed working with a broad-based group of 10 hospital employees, volunteers and medical staff. "We worked through about 20 reasons to give provided to us via a formal philanthropic stakeholder survey and a campaign feasibility study conducted by different consulting firms."

The website also features a comprehensive list of frequently asked questions that highlights reasons people might have for not wanting to give to the campaign, along with the corresponding argument for giving. Hyde says both tools are handy resources for those who are charged with asking for gifts to the capital campaign.

And, as it turns out, they also seem to be motivating for those who find the website on their own. Hyde says the campaign received one long-distance gift from a stranger — he had never before been a patient or a donor — but he did make a $50,000 gift as a direct result of the information he found on their website.

To date the campaign has raised more than $3 million, with gifts attributed to their website and contributions made online totaling more than $55,000.

Source: John Hyde, Director of Development, Texas Health Arlington Memorial Hospital, Arlington, TX.
Phone (817) 804-7278.
E-mail:
JohnHyde@TexasHealth.org

Visitors to the website for Texas Health Arlington Memorial Hospital (Arlington, TX) are greeted with this Top 10 list on reasons to support the community-owned hospital.

Content not available in this edition

Put Some Creativity Into Annual Gift Brochures

Your organization's annual giving literature plays a role in annual giving success. Yet chances are not even your most dedicated supporters eagerly anticipate reading it.

While trying to be too clever in your brochure concepts may cause potential donors to miss your point, some planning and brainstorming can pave the way to creating an annual campaign that will both attract positive attention and educate your constituency about the importance of their ongoing support.

Consider these ideas as you plan your annual campaign and publications:

✓ **Combine a brochure with a yearlong calendar.** Using a standard folded size such as 8 1/2 X 5 1/2-inch to mail in a 9 X 6-inch booklet envelope — or a format to fit a standard No. 10 business envelope — create a calendar that features a different program or service each month. List important dates related to your organization, regular holidays or even anniversaries of milestones in your history. Place detachable pledge cards or reminders in months when you hope to collect pledge installments.

✓ **Integrate nature into the concept and link it to your mission.** Animals, flowers, seasons and weather affect everyone and offer an endless list of creative possibilities for illustrating your services and values. Use illustrations, original photographs, verse or stories related to the time of year and the natural element you choose to make your points. Carry the ideas a step further with paper and ink choices. Use different shades of the same paper and a different ink color in cost-effective layouts that complement the different sections of your piece.

✓ **Use famous historical figures and children to show possibilities for your future.** Your organization has both a history and a future. Children dressed as their favorite famous person may touch people with the concept that every person, and your programs, have bright promise and possibilities ahead.

✓ **Choose a single graphic symbol that has meaning for your organization or theme.** An antique (or very modern) hourglass, decorative key, eagle, strong oak tree, race car or helping hand carry messages and images you can use as artwork for your brochure as well as related items like T-shirts and hats, and as a bridge in copy that connects the symbol with your mission. Think of the primary positive feelings you wish to convey and a visual image that can mentally connect with your audience.

✓ **A visually and verbally entertaining timeline of your immediate and future goals.** Most organizations have a long-range plan reaching beyond the current fund drive. Starting with the present, offer illustrations and text looking at your organization's future. Demonstrate how annual support is critical to fulfillment of future plans.

Even if none of these concepts is quite right for you, use them as a springboard to brainstorm with others and think of your own unique approach.

Here are five ideas for producing your organization's next annual gift brochure.